Investing Guidebook

Steven M. Bragg

AccountingTools®

ISBN-13: 978-1-64221-328-7

For more information about AccountingTools® products, visit our Web site at www.accountingtools.com.

Table of Contents

About the Author

Steven Bragg, CPA, has been the chief financial officer or controller of four companies, as well as a consulting manager at Ernst & Young. He received a master's degree in finance from Bentley College, an MBA from Babson College, and a Bachelor's degree in Economics from the University of Maine. He has been a two-time president of the Colorado Mountain Club, and is an avid alpine skier, mountain biker, and certified master diver. Mr. Bragg resides in Centennial, Colorado. He has written more than 300 books and courses, including *New Controller Guidebook*, *GAAP Guidebook*, and *Payroll Management*.

Steven maintains the accountingtools.com web site, which contains continuing professional education courses, the Accounting Best Practices podcast, and thousands of articles on accounting subjects.

Buy Additional AccountingTools Courses

AccountingTools offers more than 1,500 hours of CPE courses, with concentrations in accounting, auditing, finance, taxation, and ethics. Related courses that you might like include:

- Accounting for Investments
- Business Ratios Guidebook
- Business Valuation
- Economic Indicators
- Investing in Alternative Assets
- Real Estate Investing
- The Interpretation of Financial Statements

Go to accountingtools.com/cpe to view these additional courses.

AccountingTools®

Chapter 1
Investing Basics

Introduction

Some type of investing strategy is needed in order to build a reserve of assets for later in life. Investing well is essential if you want to retire at a reasonable age and have enough cash on hand to deal with emergencies. In the following pages, we sort through the various investment options, to determine which ones will make the most sense, given your specific circumstances.

Investing Basics

Investing is the act of allocating resources with the expectation of generating a profit. The act of investing requires two things, which are (1) setting aside enough resources to begin investing and (2) knowing what types of investments to pursue. While many investors tend to focus on the minutiae of the second step, it is important to emphasize the first one – which requires living sufficiently within your means to spin off enough cash to invest. Too often, people are tempted by the need for immediate consumption – perhaps for the latest car, television, or vacation destination – leaving no excess cash available for investment purposes.

In short, the first investing step involves maintaining and following a budget, one that sets aside sufficient cash to allow for some investing activities. If you find that the budget is too difficult to follow, then expand the expenditures somewhat, to encompass not only your basic needs but also a bit more, to keep from having to maintain an entirely monastic lifestyle. Whatever is left over is what you can use for the second investing step.

It is possible to engage in detailed analyses of investments in order to select just the right one for your needs. However, keep in mind that there is an entire industry of investment advisors that already does this – on a full-time basis. It is likely to be more cost-effective if you spend the bulk of your time working on your main professional activity, and off-load the investing decisions to an investment advisor. This does not mean abrogating all responsibility for making investment decisions, but it can mean giving the advisor parameters for where to invest (such as European stocks generally, or municipal bonds, or technology stocks in the United States), and then letting that person select the best options. In short, outsource the work that a specialist can handle for you, so that you're not spending every waking moment researching investments.

The Basic Investment Types

One of your key investment decisions is which types of investments to pursue – and which ones to avoid. In the following sub-sections, we note the general characteristics of the major investment types.

Ownership Investments

Taking an ownership stake in an investment tends to result in investment returns that are higher than the rate of inflation, resulting in above-average returns over the long term. Offsetting these returns are a higher risk of loss (since the investment vehicle may sometimes suffer major losses), as well as gyrating returns from year to year. However, if you can bear the risk of a potential loss of investment, taking an ownership interest can yield solid returns over the long term. The risk of loss can be reduced by diversifying your invested funds, to keep from putting all of your assets at risk.

<u>Stock Market Investments</u>

A common investment option is to buy the shares of publicly-held businesses. The prices of these shares are just as likely to decrease as to increase, so you may be in for a bumpy ride. If you do not want to invest too much in the shares of a single company, then another option is to buy a stock fund, which invests in clusters of shares. For example, a stock fund might invest in the shares of every stock issuer within a stock index, or only in the stocks of the technology sector, or only in the stocks of larger companies. These more dispersed holdings will shield you from large declines in the price of any individual stock, though doing so also prevents you from taking full advantage of a large run-up in the price of a single stock. Any of these investments can be made with an online brokerage account.

Generally, the way to make a reasonable return on stock market investments is to make investments in the market on a regular basis, keeping investing costs down, and restricting your investments to well-established businesses with a proven track record. Investing in startup companies is much riskier, since the chance of making a gigantic return is offset by the potential loss of your entire investment.

<u>Real Estate Investments</u>

Taking an ownership position in real estate presents the opportunity to not just profit from rent receipts, but also from the long-term appreciation of the property. Further, a large part of the funds used to invest in real estate comes from a mortgage, which means that the actual initial investment in real estate can be relatively small. This has proven to be a solid road to wealth for many investors. However, if you elect to manage properties directly (without a property manager), then real estate management can consume a large part of your time. In addition, it may be difficult to replace lost tenants, while older structures require substantial amounts of maintenance. Consequently, there is a risk that rental receipts will drop below expenditures, triggering losses. See our *Real Estate Investing* course for more information.

<u>Business Ownership Investments</u>

The most active type of ownership investment is in a business that you operate. The advantage here is that you have full control over how the business is operated, so the profits (or losses) generated are based on your decisions. This can result in significant cash flows from the business, as well as further profits from its eventual sale. A major downside of this approach is that a large part of your net worth may be tied up in the business, so if it fails, you might end up in a precarious financial position. See our *Entrepreneur's Guidebook* course for more information.

Lending Arrangements

The largest alternative to ownership investments is to lend money to other parties. We do not refer to the issuance of actual loans, but rather to putting your money into savings instruments that yield a specific return. There are two variations on the concept, as noted next.

Savings Instruments

One of the safest investment choices is to invest in a savings instrument, such as a savings account at the local bank, or a certificate of deposit. Or, you may acquire a bond[1] that has been issued by a business or government entity. When you take this approach, you are essentially lending money to the savings institution or bond issuer. As a general rule, longer-term savings instruments pay back a somewhat higher interest rate than shorter-term instruments, though the difference in rates may not be that large.

There are pluses and minuses to the use of savings instruments. One plus is that these investments tend to be quite safe, and (depending on the circumstances) might even be guaranteed by the government. The main downside is the lack of any outsized returns. You will receive the interest guaranteed by the other party, but nothing more. For example, if Amazon issues a bond that pays 4% interest and you buy it, then you will receive a 4% return over the life of the bond – and nothing more. Meanwhile, Amazon may use your money to generate a 20% return, all of which benefits its shareholders. In addition, there is a risk that the rate of inflation over the term of the investment will exceed the return from it, in which case your actual return, net of inflation, will be negative. Furthermore (with the exception of interest on municipal bonds), you will also have to pay taxes on the interest earned, which reduces your return even more.

> **Tip:** If you *must* invest in a short-term savings instrument, then put the cash into a money market account. These accounts generate a higher return than your local bank, are easy to access when you need cash, and are quite safe. Their investments must have an average maturity of less than 60 days, which minimizes their sensitivity to changes in interest rates.

---

[1] A bond is a fixed obligation to pay that is issued by a corporation or government entity to investors. Bonds are used to raise cash for operational or infrastructure projects. They usually include a periodic coupon (interest) payment, and are paid off as of a specific maturity date.

Debt Reduction

An excellent investment choice can be to pay down existing debt. This is especially the case when the debt has a high interest rate associated with it, as is the case with credit card debt. Auto loans also tend to have relatively high interest rates associated with them, and so could be paid off in order to eliminate the interest payments. A variable-rate mortgage might also be a good choice for elimination, if the rate has escalated over time. A more problematic debt reduction is a fixed-rate mortgage, if the rate is relatively low. In this case, you might be able to gain a greater return from investing funds elsewhere, rather than paying down the mortgage.

Other Investments

In the following sub-sections, we make note of several additional investing options. As we point out in the descriptions of each one, they are generally not recommended. Instead, the preceding ownership investments are generally considered to be the best choices.

Call Options

Rather than buying stock outright, it is possible to purchase a *call option* that gives you the right, but not the obligation, to buy the stock at a predetermined price within a specific range of dates. For example, you might purchase a call option that allows you to buy the shares of ABC International for $100 per share for the next six months. If the share price were to ascend from its current $90 price to $120, then it would make sense to exercise the call option, buy+ the shares for $100 each, and immediately sell them for a $20 profit per share. Offsetting this profit would be the price of the call option and any brokerage commissions.

The problem with call options is that the price of the stock might not increase to a point where it makes sense to exercise the option. If so, the option will expire, and you will have lost the amount that you spent on the option. For this reason, investing in call options is speculative, and so should be avoided.

Put Options

A *put option* is a contract that gives its holder the right, but not the obligation, to sell stock at a strike price, before the option's expiration date. This means that you can force the counterparty to buy your shares at a specific price if the market price of the stock declines. If the price of your stock holding does not decline, then the option expires unused. Put options are a risk management technique that can be used to prevent the value of your investments from falling below a targeted level.

Put options are most valuable when you want to hold shares for an extended period of time in order to take advantage of lower capital gains tax rates, but want to avoid the risk of the share price falling in value before the holding period has been completed. These options have the same problem as call options, which is that you may pay for an option and then never use it.

Precious Metals

Some investors like to keep some of their funds invested in precious metals, such as silver or gold. There is some natural demand for these metals, since they are used in manufacturing and jewelry. In addition, there is cultural demand for them in some countries, such as India, where maintaining stocks of gold is considered a reasonable investment strategy. In short, a baseline level of demand maintains a floor price for these metals, above which the market price may vary.

Investing in precious metals can yield a reasonable return during periods of uncertainty, such as when the inflation rate increases, or when there are wars. During these times, investors tend to buy more precious metals, which drives up demand and therefore its price. However, the long-term return on investment tends to be poor, and certainly lower than the other major investment classes. Rather than investing directly in precious metals, an alternative that may yield a better return is to invest in a fund that focuses on investments in companies that deal with precious metals. By doing so, you can benefit from increases in the value of these shares.

Currencies

It is possible to invest in other currencies, usually those that are considered to be stable – such as the Japanese yen or the Swiss franc. The investment logic is that you should shift your cash out of currencies that are declining in value and into stable ones, in order to benefit from relative increases in value. When you need the funds, you can convert back into your home currency at a better exchange rate, realizing a gain. This is certainly an option when the government of your country is engaging in inflationary fiscal practices, such as spending more money than it is taking in via tax receipts, and especially when it is printing new money at a rate that exceeds the growth rate of the country. For this reason, the residents of high-inflation countries routinely shift their excess cash balances into other currencies.

However, if your country of residence is *not* suffering from high inflation, then the case in favor of investing in foreign currencies is substantially less credible. The problem is that exchange rates can be moved up or down by a variety of factors that are not remotely controllable, such as the impact of bad weather on a country's economy, or investor expectations regarding the newly-elected president of a country, or changes in the interest rate that are set by its central bank. In short, unless high inflation is a factor, it is generally best to avoid investing in other currencies.

Collectibles

You might choose to invest in *collectibles*, which are items worth more than they were originally sold for, due to their rarity or popularity. Examples of collectibles are antiques, toys, coins, comic books, rare books, and stamps. As long as there is a strong market for collectibles, the prices of these items will increase. However, these increases are only based on supply and demand. If collectors become less enamored of a certain type of collectible, then demand will weaken and its price will decline – perhaps catastrophically. In short, collectibles are only valuable to collectors – they do not actually generate value on their own.

There are other concerns with collectibles. First, you may need to pay for storage, insurance, and appraisal costs. Second, it is entirely possible that the item purchased turns out to be a forgery. Third, the quality of the piece may deteriorate over time, especially if you are using sub-par storage. Finally, and most importantly, the long-term return on most collectibles is quite poor. In short, unless you are an absolute expert in regard to a particular type of collectible and love to collect it irrespective of future returns, it rarely makes sense to pour resources into this area.

Risk and Investing

The types of investing activities in which people engage is strongly influenced by their perception of risk. In many cases they place too much emphasis on avoiding lesser risks, while not doing enough to mitigate more substantial ones. In short, it is easy to misunderstand the impact of risk on your investments.

Part of the issues related to risk have to do with your sense of control over an investment. For example, you might have no concerns at all about spending $100,000 on new equipment for your business, because you are entirely in charge of the decision, and you have a very good idea of whether or not it will generate a return. Conversely, you might be petrified about paying $100,000 to purchase the bonds issued by a local city. The city might be in excellent financial condition, but your perception of risk is heightened because you have no control over the uses to which the city will put your money.

Despite these concerns, most people will take on investments that have some degree of risk associated with them, because the returns generated are generally higher. If they were to only put money into the safest investments, then the return on investment would be minimal. In short, there is a direct relationship between the risk of an investment and the return expected from it. In the following sub-sections, we discuss how to still generate reasonable returns while mitigating the associated risk.

Mitigating the Risk of a Decline in Market Value

It is not only possible but also quite likely that there will be a substantial drop in the stock market, perhaps due to a pandemic, war, or natural disaster. It is entirely possible for any funds invested in the stock market to experience an abrupt drop in value when one of these events occurs, perhaps in the range of 10 to 25 percent, though even larger drops have occurred. For example, the stock market crash of 1929 resulted in a 25% drop in the market over a span of just five days, while the financial crisis of 2008 triggered a 54% drop. Even though the stock markets are moderately well-regulated, it is still entirely possible that declines of this magnitude will occur again – based on the historical evidence, they will almost certainly occur again.

One way to deal with a stock market decline is to view it as a buying opportunity. When stock prices decline, this is an excellent time to buy. If your budget routinely spins off more cash that can be invested, then consider investing it in the stock market in small amounts on a regular basis. By doing so, you can acquire shares at low prices even in the midst of a recession that will, in all probability, generate solid returns when the market eventually returns to normal.

The preceding recommendation should be accompanied by a note of caution. Do not buy stocks when they are clearly overpriced. While it is impossible to anticipate exactly when the stock market is about to drop precipitously, it is not difficult at all to identify overpriced stocks, simply by looking at a trend of their price/earnings ratios over time. In these situations, invest your additional cash in new investments that are not clearly overpriced. This might mean investing in foreign stock markets where prices are lower, or perhaps temporarily parking the funds in lower-return debt instruments until a market correction has occurred.

If you are in need of cash and you are holding some investments that are clearly overpriced, sell these investments first (subject to tax considerations). Doing so eliminates those investments that are most at risk of declining in value.

Another way to deal with a market decline is through diversification. Invest some of your cash in overseas markets, where the triggering event might not have as much of an impact. Or, invest a portion of the funds in real estate, or perhaps in bonds. By diversifying, only a portion of your funds will be at risk from any one event. It is quite possible that, while some investments are in decline, others will appreciate, resulting in a net overall gain.

Another consideration is your investment period. If you are willing to invest over a long period of time (such as several decades), then any short-term drops in the market – however large they may be – should not cause much angst. Over the long term, the market should recover from these declines, giving you a tidy return. If your expected holding period covers a shorter period of time (as is the case for someone nearing retirement), then it might be prudent to gradually shift your funds into more stable investments, such as bonds, so that you won't have to worry about sudden drops in value. Shifting to more stable returns will likely result in lower returns, so there is a cost associated with taking this approach.

Tip: If you are uncertain about how you would feel about buying into risky investments, then consider making a small investment of this type, and monitor how you feel about it over time, as its value spikes and plunges. This will help you to understand whether a larger investment is warranted – or none at all.

Mitigating the Risk of a Decline in a Specific Investment

If you have poured your funds into a relatively small number of investments, then a decline in the value of any one of them will have a disproportionately large (and negative) impact on your total holdings. The obvious mitigation activity in these cases is to diversify into a broader range of investments. For example, if your funds are concentrated in technology stocks, consider shifting some of it to unrelated industries, such as hotels or mining. Doing so makes it less likely that an industry-wide decline will have a severe impact on your holdings.

A good way to diversify is to hire a professional to do it for you. A professional manager has a better understanding of the risks associated with investments, and knows which companies in various industries represent a good value. The fees charged for this service are well worth the resulting risk mitigation.

If your investments are concentrated in real estate, then be sure to conduct detailed due diligence on all properties that you are considering buying. This means not taking any shortcuts on inspections. A few pennies saved up front on inspections can be extremely costly over the long term, if they result in you not knowing about issues that have to be repaired at a later date.

Mitigating the Risk of Inflation

A major concern is the negative impact of inflation on your investment returns. It is entirely likely that even a modest rate of inflation will completely offset any returns generated by low-risk investments (such as government bonds). To keep this from happening, allocate a reasonable proportion of your investable funds into higher-return (and yes, riskier) investments; doing so will generate returns sufficiently high to offset the negative effects of inflation.

FDIC Coverage

We leave this section with a brief discussion of the benefits of FDIC deposit insurance coverage. The Federal Deposit Insurance Corporation (FDIC) is an independent agency created by Congress to maintain stability and public confidence in the nation's financial system. Among other functions, the FDIC insures bank deposits, so that you will not lose deposited funds in the event of a bank failure. The standard insurance amount is $250,000 per depositor, per insured bank, for each account ownership category. If you open a deposit account in an FDIC-insured bank, you are automatically covered.

What this means is that, if you insist on keeping funds in a bank, rather than in some more productive investment vehicle, then be sure to cap your deposits at each bank at $250,000. Any funds over that amount will not be insured by the FDIC. This can result in having a number of accounts scattered across several banks.

Liquidity and Investing

Liquidity is the ease with which an asset or security can be converted into cash. The liquidity of an investment is a major concern when there is a good chance that you will need to convert some investments into cash in the near term. Liquidity is a non-factor when you are primarily invested in publicly-traded stocks, since they can be easily sold off simply by stating your intention on the broker's website. Liquidity is much more of a concern when your funds are invested in real estate, since the process of listing the property, showing it to interested parties, and closing on a deal can take several months. The process takes even longer when you own a business; finding the right buyer who is willing to pay an acceptable price might take more than a year. Also, in the cases of both real estate and selling a business, selling costs can be substantial. When your funds are mostly tied up in illiquid investments, consider maintaining investments in highly liquid investments that will cover your expenses through a worst-case scenario, such as taking a year to sell your business. This type of buffer will probably offer a lower return, but the increased level of liquidity will be worth it.

Return on Investment

One of the essential elements of investment decisions is the type of investment return that you will generate. The calculation of total return has several elements associated with it. A good way to address the topic is with an example. We start with a person who wants to invest in stocks. Her total shareholder return is the profit generated from all share price appreciation (or depreciation), dividends received, and transactional costs. The calculation of her total return is as follows:

<u>(ending stock price – beginning stock price) + sum of all dividends received – transaction costs</u>
Share purchase price

The investor purchases 1,000 shares of Albatross Flight Systems for $15.00 per share, for a total investment of $15,000. She pays her brokerage $50 to conduct the transaction. A year later, the market value of the shares is $17.00, and she has received several dividends totaling $1.50 per share. Based on this information, her total shareholder return is:

<u>($17,000 ending price - $15,000 beginning price) + $1,500 dividends - $50 brokerage fee</u>
$15,000 purchase price

=23% total shareholder return

Alternatively, what about the return on investment when you park cash in a savings account at a bank? The interest paid on these accounts tends to be quite low, perhaps just a few percent. If the bank pays monthly interest on the account, this means that the interest is compounding. Compounded interest is being paid when the monthly interest payment is loaded back into your savings account by the bank, which then pays interest on the interest. Depending on the compounding frequency, compounded interest can have a noticeable impact on your return on investment. The formula used to calculate compound interest is as follows:

$$A = P\left(1 + \frac{r}{n}\right)^{nt}$$

Where:

A = Total accumulated money (principal plus interest)
P = Principal
r = Interest rate stated as a decimal
n = Number of times that compounding occurs during the year
t = Number of years

It is easier to calculate compound interest using the future value function in Excel, for which the formula is:

$$=FV(rate,nper,pmt,pv)$$

The Excel calculation is explained in more detail as follows:

=FV (interest rate, total number of periods, fixed payment amount
to be made in each period (if any), and the initial payment amount,
stated as a negative)

For example, an investor puts $25,000 into a savings account at the beginning of the year, earning 4% interest, compounded monthly. How much money is in the account at the end of the year? The calculation is as follows:

$$=FV(0.00333,12,0,-25000)$$

$$= \$26,017.50$$

$$=4.07\% \text{ return on investment}$$

Since we are using 12 compounding periods in the formula, the 4% interest rate must be divided by 12 to get the 0.00333 interest rate used in the formula.

When computing the return on investment, an additional concern is the impact of taxes. Federal income taxes will apply, and possibly also state income taxes – depending on where you live. For example, a relatively wealthy investor living in California can expect to pay about a 35% federal income tax and a 10% state tax. While income tax rates will decline when investments have been held for protracted periods, the impact of taxes on investments is still substantial.

Summary

If there is one lesson to be learned from this chapter, it is that risk is tied to reward, so higher-return investments also present the risk of volatile earnings, and possibly of the loss of your investment. That being the case, the essential question to ask yourself is what level of risk are you willing to tolerate? If you cannot sleep well at night, knowing that your invested funds could be lost the next day, then scale back to a more tolerable risk-return profile that works for you. Generally, younger people have a higher risk tolerance, since they have more years in which to weather the vagaries of their investments, while older people want to lock in their funds for retirement without having to worry about investment losses. Wealthier people can also afford to take more risk, since they can carve out a portion of their savings for riskier investments, while still preserving a chunk of their wealth with safer investment vehicles.

Chapter 2
Baseline Investing Activities

Introduction

Before worrying too much about whether to invest in foreign stocks or perhaps in the advanced technology sector, you should first ensure that your baseline investing activities are in order. Once they have been settled, you can look further afield for investing opportunities. In this chapter, we address the most basic investing considerations.

Step 1. Create a Cash Reserve

All types of disasters can arise over the years, such as a hailstorm damaging your roof, a broken pipe flooding the basement, or being unexpectedly fired from a well-paying job (and that just covers the items that have impacted the author!). If you have every last dime invested in real estate or some other long-term investment, then these situations can trigger a major scramble to find cash. To keep these issues from having too great of a negative impact on your life, the first step in establishing baseline investing activities is to park enough cash in a savings or money market account to cover your expenses for the next three to six months. It is easy to withdraw cash from these investment vehicles, and they do not lose value. While these investments will not generate much of a return, they *will* provide you with a significant amount of security.

If you are waffling over whether to establish a cash reserve, consider the costs that you will incur to obtain the cash by other means. For example, if a medical emergency requires you to cough up $50,000, will you have to sell your house to obtain the funds, or take out a loan against your 401(k) plan, or perhaps borrow it from siblings? Are these viable options?

Step 2. Obtain Adequate Insurance

We will continue with the theme of being conservative in setting up financial backstops in case of emergencies. Now that a cash reserve is in place, the next step is to obtain adequate insurance to protect you from major losses. This certainly includes insurance that covers your major medical expenses. It is fine to obtain insurance that requires a large deductible, since the point is not to cover *all* of your medical bills – only the massive ones that might otherwise bankrupt you. Also obtain liability insurance to protect against lawsuits, which might otherwise result in your assets being sold off to pay a successful litigant. Further, obtain enough life insurance to protect the livelihoods of any dependents in case you die.

If you own a business, then protect its assets by obtaining commercial general liability insurance, property insurance, and other insurance as recommended by your insurance broker. If the company is publicly-held, then a likely addition will be directors and officers liability insurance.

> **Tip:** We are not implying that you should obtain comprehensive insurance coverage in all possible areas. Instead, focus on protecting against catastrophic losses. There is no need to spend extra money on insurance to protect against lesser losses.

Step 3. Reduce Debt

The next baseline investing activity is to pay down your debts, with an emphasis on eliminating all high-interest debt. The advantage here is the outright certainty of being able to eliminate high-cost debt, versus the possibility of perhaps earning an equally generous return on high-risk investments. When in doubt, always take the certainty of eliminating debt.

When paying down debt, the top priority should always be credit cards, since they charge the highest interest rates – frequently in the vicinity of 20%. Next in priority should be any other consumer debt, such as car loans. While these loans have lower interest rates associated with them, the trade-off between paying down debt and using the money for investments is still an easy one. Once again, compare the certainty of a debt payoff versus the much less certain possibility of earning more money (after taxes) from risky investments.

The situation is not so clear for your home mortgage. The interest rate tends to be fairly low, and the interest expense is tax deductible. However, if you are holding a variable-rate mortgage, then you are at considerable risk of having the interest rate escalate over time. When this situation exists, you should seriously consider either paying down the mortgage or refinancing into a fixed-rate mortgage. This is also a good choice when you are nervous about being liable for a large amount of debt.

The key issue when deciding whether to pay down your mortgage is the nature of what you would otherwise do with the money. If you plan to invest it in high-risk, high-return investments, such as real estate or the stock market, then doing so makes sense. However, if you instead plan to park the money in a savings account that earns minimal interest, then that is a worse use of your money than just paying down the mortgage.

Step 4. Budget a Savings Rate

Start tracking your income and spending on a spreadsheet, listing this information for multiple periods. Doing so gives you a good idea of your spending habits. This will also tell you how much money you have left over at the end of the month (or how much additional debt you have taken on).

Assuming that you have some excess cash left over at the end of most months, think about whether it is large enough to help you achieve your lifetime goals (such as founding a business, or traveling the world, or retiring at 50). If this cash flow is relatively small and your goals are large, then the only way to meet your goals will be to invest in high-risk, high-return investments. There is simply no other way to build up enough cash. Alternatively, if you are lucky enough to be spinning off a lot of cash, then this comparison might instead allow you to invest a bit more safely in lower-return, lower-risk investments that will still allow you to achieve your goals.

If – as is likely for most of us – the amount of excess cash produced each month is lower than you need, then you have only two choices, which are to cut back on expenses or increase your income. Cutting back on expenses is entirely within your control, while increasing your income tends to be a chancier proposition. Consequently, the usual choice is to establish a budget for what you can and cannot do each month. Perhaps you can only dine out once a month, or only buy second-hand cars, or rent a somewhat smaller apartment. If you elect to work longer hours in order to generate more income, then this has its own cost, which is a reduced quality of life. In short, producing more investable cash will require some hard choices.

Step 5. Align Your Life and Financial Goals

At this point, your baseline financial issues have been covered, and you have some extra cash available for investing purposes. Stop! Before investing any of it, think hard about how to match your life goals with your financial goals. For example, if you plan to be a college professor until retirement, then you probably want to invest in long-term investments that will pay off years in the future. On the other hand, if you plan to quit your day job and start your own business within a few years, then it will make more sense to preserve the value of your investments over the short term and aim for more liquidity, so that you will have the cash available when it is needed. In the former case, investing in real estate and/or the stock market might make the most sense. In the latter case, parking the cash in a money market fund might be the better path to follow.

Step 6. Factor in Your Tax Situation

Don't start investing yet! You still need to take into consideration your tax situation. The incremental amount that you are taxed by the federal government varies, depending on your income. The following exhibit contains tax rates and the taxable income brackets to which they apply for a single filer in 2023.

2025 Tax Brackets for Single Filers

Tax Rate	Taxable Income Bracket
10%	$0 to $11,925
12%	$11,925 to $48,475
22%	$48,475 to $103,350
24%	$103,350 to $197,300
32%	$197,300 to $250,525
35%	$250,525 to $626,350
37%	$626,350 or more

As noted in the preceding exhibit, you are taxed at a relatively low rate on your first few dollars of income, after which the rate increases for each additional tranche of income earned. For example, if your base salary is $150,000 and you want to start investing your excess cash, then the tax rate that applies to any investment income earned will be 24%. Alternatively, if your base salary is $75,000, then the applicable tax rate for investment purposes will be 22%. These rates are your *marginal tax rate*, which means that they will apply to each incremental dollar earned. When you have a high marginal tax rate, this is a strong incentive for you to invest as much as possible in tax-protected retirement accounts, where there is no immediate tax deduction that will cut into your net income.

In addition to the federal income tax rate, you will also need to understand the impact of any gains from the sale of stocks, mutual funds, and other capital assets. The applicable tax depends on a combination of your taxable income and how long you have held the assets. Gains from the sale of capital assets that have been held for at least one year (which are classified as long-term capital gains) are taxed at either a 0%, 15%, or 20% rate. The amount of your income determines which tax rate will apply, as noted in the following exhibit.

2025 Capital Gains Tax Brackets for Single Filers

Capital Gains Rate	Taxable Income Bracket
0%	$0 to $44,625
15%	$44,626 to $492,300
20%	$492,301 or more

The tax rate on shorter-term capital gains (those assets held for less than one year) is identical to your marginal tax rate, which (as noted earlier) can range from 10% to 37%, depending on your income level.

Based on the preceding tax tables, it should be evident that the government will take a substantial chunk out of the investment earnings of higher-income investors. If this situation applies to you, then your investment strategy might want to include tax-free money markets funds or tax-free government bonds. These investments tend to have lower yields than other investments, but their tax-free status might give you better after-tax income than would have been the case with taxable investments. Other options are to invest in real estate or a business, because any gains resulting from them are only taxable after they have been sold. These types of assets may never be sold, in which case the related taxes are deferred. In addition, you can roll the profits from the sale of real estate into the purchase of a similar property, which continues to defer the related taxes. Finally, anyone in a high tax bracket should always hold onto an investment for at least a year, in order to take advantage of the lower capital gains rate. For example, a very high-income investor who sells an investment would pay a 37% federal income tax rate on it if it were sold within one year, and only a 20% rate if it were held for at least a year.

Step 7. Contribute to a Retirement Account

If you have a tax-advantaged retirement account, then maximize your contributions to it. For example, if you have a 401(k) or SEP-IRA retirement plan, then the income taxes normally paid on your earnings are deferred in the amount of your contributions into it. These amounts are only taxed once you reach retirement age and start to draw money out of the plan. This is a particularly excellent investment when you still have many years until retirement, since the deferral of tax payments will be prolonged. To enhance the situation even more, the tax rate at which you eventually pay for these earnings will be the rate you pay at retirement, when your income will presumably be lower – which puts you in a lower tax bracket.

The tax benefits associated with a retirement account are particularly large if you start contributing to it as early in life as possible. By doing so, the earnings generated by your contributions will be compounded tax-free for many years, which can result in tens or even hundreds of thousands of dollars of additional earnings until you reach retirement age.

There are several types of pension plans that an employer may offer. Participants in these plans may have a number of different investment options, which have varying risk profiles and possible returns on investment. The more common plans are as follows:

- *401(k) plan.* This is an investment account into which employees contribute funds, sometimes with additional matching funds contributed by the employer. The funds contributed by the employer are usually under a vesting arrangement, where the participants earn the funds by staying employed with the company for a certain period of time. Participants pay income taxes on the funds in a 401(k) account when they withdraw funds from the account. The net effect of a 401(k) is to defer the recognition of taxable income until retirement, when participants will presumably also be in a lower tax bracket, and so will pay fewer income taxes. With some hardship-based exceptions, a participant cannot withdraw funds from a 401(k) account until at least age 59½ without facing large penalties. To mitigate this problem for cash-strapped participants, a 401(k) account may provide for loans to participants up to the amount of their contributed funds, and on which they must pay interest.
- *Roth 401(k).* This is similar to a 401(k) account, except that the participant pays taxes on funds when they are contributed to the account, rather than when the funds are later withdrawn. By doing so, all interest earned subsequent to placing funds in the account is tax-free.
- *403(b) plan.* This is a plan similar in concept and tax treatment to the 401(k) plan, but designed for public education and non-profit entities.
- *Money purchase plan.* This plan requires the employer to pay into each employee's plan account a percentage of his or her compensation for that year. The payments can be quite substantial, since the contribution cap per year is the lesser of 25% of employee compensation or $70,000 (in 2025). These

payments are treated as deferred income for participants until they withdraw the funds.

- *Profit sharing plan.* This plan is essentially the same as a money purchase plan, except that the employer funds any contributions with a portion of its profits. The amount of payments made is discretionary, and the employer can even choose to make contributions to the plan in the absence of company profits. Contributions are typically made to each participant's account based on his or her annual compensation as a percentage of all compensation among plan participants. The contribution per year per participant is the lesser of 25% of employee compensation or $70,000 (in 2025).

We cover individual retirement accounts in the next chapter.

Note: While we are on the subject of tax-advantaged investments, it may make sense to put money into a Section 529 plan. A 529 plan helps to pay for education, including K-12 and college. A 529 savings plan can grow on a tax-deferred basis, and withdrawals are tax-free if they are used for qualified education expenses. Alternatively, a 529 prepaid tuition plan allows the account owner to pay in advance for tuition at designated colleges and universities, locking in the cost of today's education fees.

Step 8. Consider a Mix of Investments

It rarely makes sense to concentrate your holdings on a very small number of investments. Yes, one of them may turn out to have scintillating returns, but it is more likely that a single poor investment will cause your overall return on investment to be quite poor, if not negative. A better approach is to adopt a diversified investment portfolio, so that a loss on one investment is offset by gains elsewhere. For example, it can make sense to put some of your funds in technology stocks, but not all of your funds. Instead, spread the cash around among different, unrelated industries, so that a sudden drop that impacts one industry will not impact another industry in which you also have holdings.

Tip: Don't diversify too much. If you are invested in dozens of investments, it will be hard to keep track of them all. Instead, work with an investment advisor to establish a reasonably-sized group of investments that does not take too much time to monitor.

The mix of investments that you adopt should change as you age. At a younger age, there are still so many years to go until retirement that it is relatively safe to invest in higher-earning and higher-risk investments, on the grounds that there will still be plenty of time for these investments to recover their value. This is not the case as you approach retirement age, which is why it is prudent to start shifting a portion of your invested funds into more stable investments (which unfortunately also have a lower rate of return). A common rule for how much money to put into growth investments is to subtract your age from 120. For example, if you are 30 years old, then 90% of your funds should be allocated to growth investments. Conversely, if you are 65 years old, then 55% of your funds should be allocated in this manner. Interestingly, this rule also implies that you should *never* shift all of your funds into conservative investments, since no one lives to be 120 years old (as of this writing, the oldest person in the world is 116 years old, so even that person should invest 1% in growth investments!). The point being that someone entering retirement is not certain about how long he or she might live, and so should still invest moderately aggressively through a smaller proportion of the total remaining funds.

Tip: When you retire, you will probably have a mix of tax-advantaged retirement accounts and other investments. It generally makes sense to invest more aggressively through the retirement accounts for as long as possible, while drawing down the other accounts first. The reason is that the retirement accounts either defer or completely avoid taxes, so you will experience more tax advantages from growing these funds.

The same approach to adjusting your mix of investments over time can be applied to paying for a child's college expenses. You could put most of your college-designated investments into high-growth investments when college is still a number of years away, and then adjust the mix as college approaches, in order to lock in the amount of cash that will be available when it is time to pay for college.

Step 9. Consider When to Invest

Before finally initiating your investment strategy, the final consideration is when to invest. This is a particular concern when the market appears to be overheated, when there is some risk that you might be buying near the top of the market. This is a concern not just when investing in the stock market, but also when buying real estate or a business. While it might seem reasonable to just park your cash in a money market account and wait for conditions to improve, the reality is a bit different. The problem is that conditions might continue in their supposedly overheated condition, perhaps establishing a new normal. If so, you might be left behind by the market, and end up having to buy in at an even higher price at a later date.

One way to avoid this situation is to employ *dollar cost averaging*, where you invest funds at a steady rate, using consistent timing. For example, Molly inherits $1,000,000 from her parents. Stock market valuations appear to be quite high, so she is uncertain about whether to invest now, or to wait for market prices to decline. Her investment advisor suggests that she use dollar cost averaging, where she invests $250,000 in growth stocks once a quarter, with the rest of her funds invested in a money market account. By doing so, she will invest the money over a period of 12 months, through what will probably be a series of market swings. This approach will certainly keep her from investing at the top of the market, but will also prevent her from participating in some of the investment gains that might occur over the next year. Given this limitation, it generally makes more sense to employ dollar cost averaging when you are initially investing a large part of your net worth, and do not want to take a chance on losing a good chunk of it. It is also more worthwhile to use when your planned investments will be in higher-risk investments. However, if you are planning to invest a small amount of your net worth in conservative investments, then it is probably not worthwhile to use dollar cost averaging.

> **Tip:** If you plan to use dollar cost averaging, the period employed should not exceed two years. Otherwise, the odds are good that you will miss a significant upswing in asset prices.

A slight variation on the dollar cost averaging concept is called *value averaging*. Under this approach, you would buy more shares when prices are falling, and fewer shares when prices are increasing. For example, Molly invests $5,000 in an international stock fund that specializes in the European biomedical industry. The price of the fund then drops by 20%, leaving Molly with a $4,000 investment. Under value averaging, Molly would not only invest another $5,000 in the next quarter, but also an additional $1,000 to offset the decline in value. Alternatively, if her investment had increased by $1,000, then she only would have invested $4,000 in the following quarter. This approach tends to improve returns over the long term, since Molly ends up owning more shares. However, it also requires her to have enough fortitude to buy shares when prices are falling.

Step 10. Think Through the Consequences of an Asset Sale

There are several issues to consider before selling an asset. First, do you really need to? The goal for most investors should be to hold onto investments for a number of years. If you are being pressed to sell an asset by someone who is not an authority on this topic, then think again. A second consideration is whether you are approaching retirement age, and so want to reduce the variability of your investment portfolio. This makes sense, and usually means selling a portion of your stock holdings and using the resulting funds to buy bonds. The same advice applies to a portfolio that is excessively concentrated in one or two assets. If so, sell off a good portion of these assets and use the funds to diversify your holdings more broadly.

A third consideration when contemplating a stock sale is taxes. This is primarily a concern when your investments are not within a tax-deferred retirement plan. In this situation, consider selling longer-term holdings first, so that you are only paying the lower capital gains tax. It is also worthwhile to specify exactly which stocks are to be sold, so that you sell the ones for which you paid the most; this results in the lowest total profit. If you do not make this specification to your brokerage firm, the IRS will assume that you sold those stocks that you acquired earliest, which may result in larger taxable profits.

> **Tip:** If you expect your tax rate to decline in the future – as commonly happens when you retire – then hold off on selling stocks for which you've generated the most profits, until you are in that lower tax bracket.

If you are planning to sell some assets for which there will be associated losses, consider also selling some assets for which there will be a roughly comparable gain. Doing so offsets the gains and losses, resulting in no tax at all.

When planning to sell securities, it is useful to be aware of the *wash sale rule*. This rule states that a taxpayer cannot claim a loss on the sale or trade of a security if it is replaced with a substantially identical security within 30 days. This rule is intended to prevent investors from manufacturing losses for tax purposes on securities that they are essentially continuing to hold. The specifics of the wash sale rule are as follows:

- A wash sale is considered to be any transaction where a security is disposed of and then within 30 days is replaced or the taxpayer acquires an option or contract to replace the security.
- The rule applies if a spouse or an entity controlled by the individual obtains the replacement security.
- The 30-day rule involves 30 calendar days, not 30 business days (which would span a longer period of time).
- Any loss on the sale of the initial security is added to the cost basis of the replacement security.
- The holding period of the initial security is added to the holding period of the replacement security, which likely results in a long-term holding period.
- Any security is subject to the wash sale rule if it has a CUSIP number (a unique identifier for stocks and bonds).

As an example, an investor buys 1,000 shares of Higgins Electric on October 1 for $25,000. On October 15, the value of the 1,000 shares has dropped to $22,000, so the investor sells all of the shares to realize a loss of $3,000 on her tax return. On October 28, she repurchases the 1,000 shares. In this case, the initial loss cannot be counted as a tax loss, since the shares were repurchased within such a short period of time.

> **Tip:** To sidestep the wash sale rule, always schedule security repurchases for at least 31 days after the sale date. Or, if you have sold a mutual fund or exchange-traded fund for a loss, then just buy into a similar fund with the proceeds, rather than the same fund.

A Note Regarding Information Sources

There is a massive amount of financial advice available from many sources. This advice may come from newsletters, online articles, podcasts, and acquaintances. How can you sort through it all, to decide how to invest? A good first rule is to figure out how the information source is making money. For example, if the source is a web page that you have accessed for free, then you are the author's revenue source. This may mean that the web page is blanketed with advertising, or there is a link to an online course, or they want you to contact one of their brokers, or perhaps the website is tracking your online habits, which it then sells to a third party. The point is that no one is giving you advice for free – they want to make money from you. That being the case, be careful about taking advice from these sources.

> **Tip:** Be especially careful when reading the content on investing websites that use advertising. These organizations are posting content that is specifically targeted at convincing you to buy the advertiser's product – which may be a seminar on how to invest in an activity that is against your best interests. They may also specifically state the benefits of investing with their advertisers – which may not be a good idea at all.

A good second rule is that, if you are directly paying for the advice (as is the case with an investment advisor), then there is no question about the motivations of the other party – you are paying them to help you. This may be expensive, but it is a more honest relationship.

A very useful third rule is to understand the other party's agenda. This is especially useful when dealing with salespeople. If they work on a commission basis, then their goal is to convince you to buy – even if doing so is not in your best interests. Similarly, if they are expressing outrageous claims for investment returns in their newsletter, they are trying to convince you to keep subscribing. On the other hand, if they work on a salaried basis, then it is much more likely that they genuinely want to help you, since they will gain no financial reward from talking to you.

> **Tip:** Assume that the historical return on investment claims stated by anyone contacting you are wrong, unless those claims have been proven by an independent audit – which is almost never the case.

Finally, gain a solid background in how investing works and how to develop a disciplined approach that works for you (such as by reading this course). By developing this baseline level of knowledge, you will be in a better position to understand which advice is right for you, and which advice is to be avoided.

Summary

The topics covered in this chapter were intended to provide a structure for your investing activities. The basic steps were to first ensure that you are covered against emergency situations that could negatively impact your finances, after which you target "low hanging fruit" to make the most use of your available dollars. Once these issues are covered, the next steps are to gather information about how much money will be available to invest, how much of a rate of return to target, the extent to which taxes will impact your returns, what mix of investments to use, and when to start making investments. With these organizational issues out of the way, we will now turn to actual investing activities – starting in the next chapter with individual retirement accounts.

Chapter 3
Individual Retirement Accounts

Introduction

Individual retirement accounts (IRAs) are among the most heavily-used retirement vehicles in the United States. These accounts are designed to defer the recognition of income that has been contributed to an account, so that the income can be recognized during one's retirement, when a person is presumably in a lower tax bracket. In this chapter, we discuss the various types of IRAs, caps on contributions to them, the deductibility of these contributions, required minimum distributions, and several related topics.

Overview of Individual Retirement Accounts

The reporting requirements for a qualified retirement plan are substantial, so a smaller employer may not want to invest the amount of staff time and money in maintaining one. An alternative is to encourage employees to create their own personal retirement accounts. There are many types of these accounts, of which the more popular are noted in the following subsections.

Individual Retirement Account (IRA)

An individual retirement account is also referred to as a traditional IRA. This is an account that a person creates, and into which he or she can contribute the lower of total annual compensation or (as of 2025) $7,000 per year, or $8,000 for those at least 50 years old. Depending upon the circumstances, these contributions may be tax deductible for those employees with lower compensation levels. In addition, any income earned on the funds invested in it is shielded from taxation until withdrawn. A person can begin withdrawing funds from the account as of age 59½, and is required to begin doing so as of age 73. If a person does not withdraw the minimum required amount as of age 73, the penalty for not doing so is 50% of the amount that should have been withdrawn.

A variation on the concept is the individual retirement annuity. This account is opened by buying an annuity contract from a life insurance company. In order to be classified as an IRA, the owner's interest in the contract must be nonforfeitable. Further, the contract must provide that the owner cannot transfer any part of it to another person. There must also be flexible premiums, so that payments can be altered if the owner's compensation changes. Also, the contract must state that contributions cannot be more than the deductible amount for an IRA, and that any refunded premiums must be used to pay for future premiums or buy more benefits before the end of the year following the year in which a refund was received.

Roth IRA

This is similar to a traditional IRA account, except that the participant pays taxes on funds when they are contributed to the account, rather than when the funds are later withdrawn. By doing so, all interest earned subsequent to placing funds in the account is tax-free. A participant can withdraw funds from the account as of age 59½. Since there is no subsequent taxation of the earnings in a Roth IRA, there is no reason for the government to require participants to draw down these funds, so there is no minimum draw down, as was the case for a traditional IRA. Instead, no withdrawal is required from this account until the death of the owner. Once the account owner dies, the same minimum distribution rules that apply to traditional IRAs also apply to Roth IRAs.

The following table shows the scenarios under which it is possible to make contributions to a Roth IRA.

Ability to Contribute to a Roth IRA

Filing Status	Modified Adjusted Gross Income	Contribution Status
Married filing jointly	Less than $236,000	Up to $7,000 ($8,000 if age 50 or older)
	At least $236,000 but less than $246,000	Reduced contribution
	$246,000+	No contribution allowed
Married filing separately, and lived with spouse at any time during the year	Zero	Up to $7,000 ($8,000 if age 50 or older)
	More than zero but less than $10,000	Reduced contribution
	$10,000	No contribution allowed
Single, head of household, or married filing separately and did not live with your spouse at any time during the year	Less than $150,000	Up to $7,000 ($8,000 if age 50 or older)
	At least $150,000 but less than $165,000	Reduced contribution
	$165,000+	No contribution allowed

IRA and Roth IRA Comparison

Some of the differences and similarities between traditional and Roth IRAs are noted in the following exhibit.

Comparison of Traditional and Roth IRAs

Features	Traditional IRA	Roth IRA
Who is allowed to contribute?	Anyone with taxable compensation	Anyone with taxable compensation and a modified adjusted gross income below a predetermined cap
Can contributions be deducted?	Qualifying contributions are deductible	Contributions are not deductible
How much can be contributed?	The combined amount for both IRAs is the smaller of $7,000 (or $8,000 for someone age 50 or older), or one's taxable compensation for the year.	
What is the contribution deadline?	The tax return filing deadline, not including any extensions.	
When can money be withdrawn?	Money can be withdrawn at any time.	
Is a minimum distribution required?	The account owner must begin taking distributions by April 1 following the year in which he or she turned age 73, and by December 31 of subsequent years.	Not required for the original owner of the account.
Are withdrawals taxable?	All deductible contributions and earnings that are withdrawn are taxable. If a withdrawal is made prior to age 59½, a 10% tax may be imposed.	A qualified distribution is not taxable. A distribution is qualified when it is made after the five-year period beginning with the first tax year for which a contribution was made to the account, *and* the distribution was made after reaching age 59½, or was made due to being disabled, or for a first-time home purchase, or was made to a beneficiary or estate due to the account owner's death. Otherwise, a 10% tax may be imposed.

In the last row of the preceding exhibit, we noted a number of situations in which a distribution from a Roth IRA is considered to be a qualified distribution. The flowchart in the following exhibit clarifies when this is the case.

Qualified Distribution Criteria for a Roth IRA

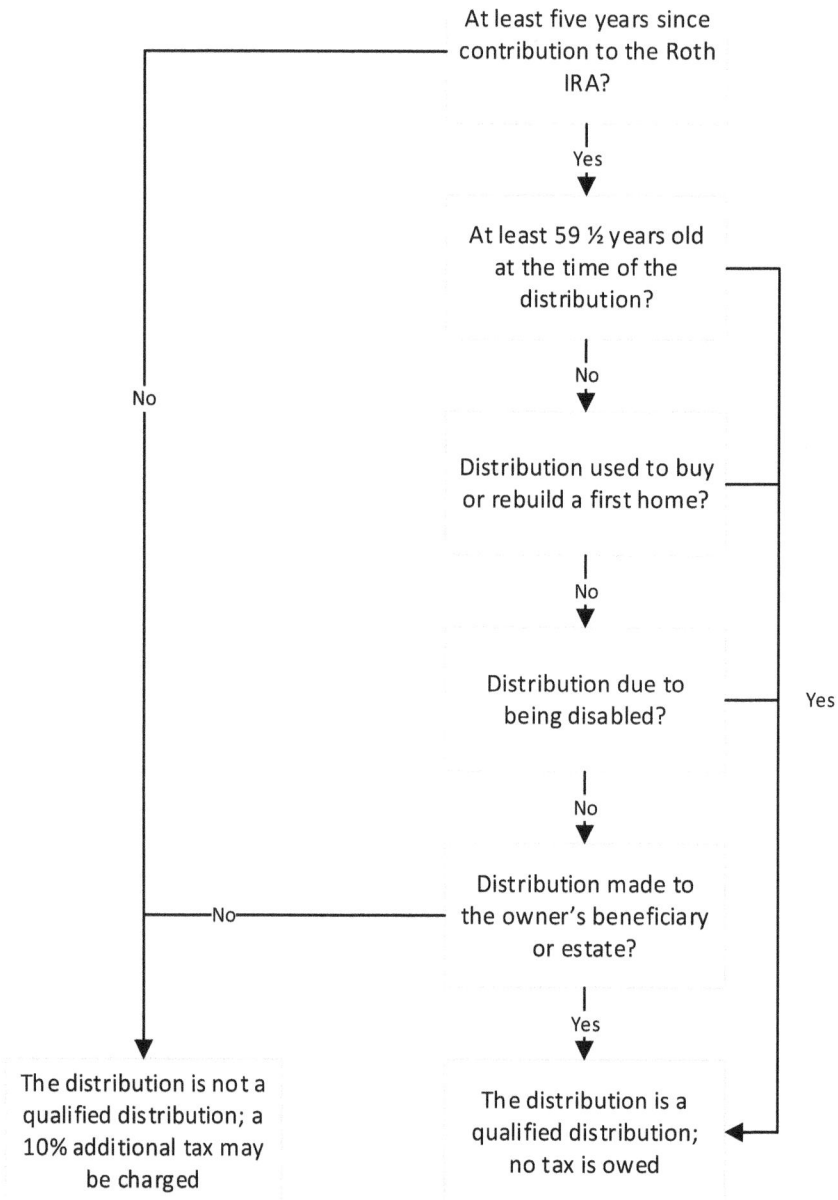

At least five years since contribution to the Roth IRA?

| Yes

At least 59 ½ years old at the time of the distribution?

| No

Distribution used to buy or rebuild a first home?

| No

Distribution due to being disabled?

| No

Distribution made to the owner's beneficiary or estate?

| Yes

No

Yes

No

The distribution is not a qualified distribution; a 10% additional tax may be charged

The distribution is a qualified distribution; no tax is owed

Rollover IRA

When an employee leaves a business where he or she has funds in a qualified pension plan, the best options are to either leave the funds in the plan, roll them into the qualified plan of the new employer, or roll them into a rollover IRA. This last option is an IRA account that is specifically designed to accept funds from qualified pension plans.

Since many people have multiple employers during their careers, many with qualified pension plans, it makes sense to consolidate the funds in these accounts into a rollover IRA.

Savings Incentive Match Plan for Employees (SIMPLE)

As the acronym implies, this is a simplified retirement plan under which both the employer and employee can make contributions to an IRA account. It is funded through a pre-tax reduction of employee gross pay. The maximum annual contribution to a SIMPLE account (as of 2025) was $16,500 and $20,000 for those at least 50 years old. A SIMPLE plan can only be created by an employer having fewer than 100 employees, or which has employed an average of 100 or fewer employees in either of the two preceding years. If a business subsequently increases its employment, it can still operate a SIMPLE plan as long as it does not employ an average of 100 or more people in a subsequent year. This plan requires the employer to match each employee's salary reduction contribution on a dollar-for-dollar basis up to 3% of the employee's compensation. A variation is the nonelective contribution, where the employer can choose to make a 2%-of-compensation contribution on behalf of each eligible employee, even if the employees do not elect to make a salary deduction into their IRA accounts.

EXAMPLE

Alvin, an employee of Universal Routers, earned $60,000 and elected to defer 5% of his salary by contributing it to a SIMPLE IRA. The company makes a standard 3% match to all such contributions. This means that Alvin contributes $3,000 to the account (calculated as $60,000 × 5%), while the company contributes $1,800 (calculated as $60,000 × 3%).

If a participant wants to withdraw funds from a SIMPLE account before age 59½, the penalty is 10% of the distribution, or 25% if the withdrawal occurs within two years of beginning participation in the plan.

When a SIMPLE plan is set up, a separate IRA account must be created for each participating employee. Participating employees are those who received at least $5,000 in compensation during any two years preceding the current calendar year, and who are reasonably expected to receive at least that much during the current calendar year.

Simplified Employee Pension (SEP) IRA

This plan is designed for the self-employed person, but can be extended to all types of business entities. A SEP IRA can only be created if there is no qualified retirement plan already in place. Contributions to a SEP IRA are protected from income taxes until such time as they are withdrawn from the account. Participants may begin withdrawing funds from the account as of age 59½, and must make required minimum distributions once they reach age 73. The total contribution to a SEP IRA cannot exceed the lesser of 25% of a participant's annual compensation or $70,000 (as of 2025).

These contribution levels make the SEP IRA one of the best ways to protect a substantial amount of funds from taxation.

EXAMPLE

Martha earned $48,000 in 2025. The maximum contribution she can make to her SEP IRA is $12,000 (calculated as 25% × $48,000).

EXAMPLE

Mary earned $300,000 in 2025. The maximum contribution she can make to her SEP IRA is $70,000, since that is the maximum allowable contribution for 2025.

Someone who is eligible for a SEP IRA must be at least 21 years old, has worked for the business in at least three of the past five years, and has received at least $600 of compensation from the business in the past year.

Contributions to a SEP IRA must be in cash; contributions of property are not allowed.

> **Note:** If SEP contributions exceed the annual deduction limit, the excess can be carried forward and used in a later year. However, an excess contribution can be subject to a 10% excise tax.

Ability to Contribute to an IRA

Anyone can make contributions to a traditional IRA if they received taxable compensation during the year. This is the case even if a taxpayer is already covered by another retirement plan. However, when there *is* another retirement plan, it may not be possible to deduct all contributions made to the IRA.

As long as both spouses in a marriage are earning compensation, each one can open an IRA. However, they cannot both participate in the same IRA; each person must maintain a separate account. If the two file a joint return, then only one spouse needs to have compensation for both of them to contribute to an IRA.

> **Note:** The compensation from which IRA contributions can be made include wages, salaries, commissions, alimony, combat pay, and graduate study income. It does *not* include earnings from property, interest and dividend income, pension or annuity income, deferred compensation, or any amounts excluded from taxable income.

Even someone participating in an employer-sponsored retirement plan (such as a SIM-PLE IRA or SEP IRA) can contribute to a traditional IRA or Roth IRA. However, as noted in a following section, these contributions may not be deductible.

Contributions to an IRA can be made at any time during the year, or by the due date for filing one's return for that year, not including extensions. For example, a contribution made for 2024 must usually be made by April 15, 2025. If a contribution is made to an IRA between January 1 and April 15, the account sponsor must be told the year to which the contribution is to be applied. If the account owner does not make this designation, then the account sponsor will report to the IRS that it was made for the current year.

Caps on IRA Contributions

The contribution caps for singles and spouses are noted in the following sub-sections, as well as the treatment of excess contributions.

Contribution Caps for Singles

The general cap rule on IRA contributions is the smaller of a person's taxable compensation or $7,000 ($8,000 if the person is at least 50 years old).

EXAMPLE

Alvin is 37 years old and single. He earned $39,000 in the past year. His IRA contribution is capped at $7,000 in that year.

Margot is 25 and single. She earned $2,000 while working on a part-time basis in the past year. Her IRA contribution is capped at $2,000 (her compensation) in that year.

If a person invests in an individual retirement annuity, then the amount that can be contributed towards its cost is capped at $7,000 per year ($8,000 if the person is at least 50 years old). A larger contribution will disqualify the annuity contract.

Contribution Caps for Spouses

Both spouses can contribute to their own separate IRAs when they file a joint return and have taxable compensation. The most that can be contributed for the year to a spouse's IRA is the lesser of the following amounts:

- $7,000 (or $8,000 if the person is at least 50 years old); or
- The total compensation includible in the gross income of both spouses, less the other spouse's IRA contribution for the year to a traditional IRA and any contributions for the year to a Roth IRA on behalf of your spouse.

It does not matter which spouse earned the income. These rules mean that the maximum contribution that can be made for the year by both spouses is $16,000, if both are at least 50 years old.

EXAMPLE

Victoria marries Albert. Albert has no taxable income (being a medical student), while Victoria earns $300,000 a year as an investment banker. Both are in their 20s. Victoria plans to contribute $7,000 to a traditional IRA. If they file a joint return, each one can contribute $7,000 to a traditional IRA. This is because Albert, who earns no income, can add Victoria's compensation, reduced by the amount of her IRA contribution ($293,000) to his own compensation to calculate his maximum contribution to a traditional IRA.

If a person contributes less than the maximum amount to a traditional IRA in one year, it is not possible to contribute an additional amount after the due date of that year's tax return in order to make up the difference.

Excess Contributions

When an excess contribution is made to a traditional IRA, it is subject to a 6% tax. This tax must be paid every year on excess amounts that remain in the account at the end of the tax year. No tax is due as long as the excess amount and any interest earned on it is withdrawn from the account by the date the tax return for that year is due, including extensions.

EXAMPLE

Irma has mistakenly made an excess contribution to her IRA of $1,000. She does not withdraw these funds by the time her tax return is due, so she owes a $60 (6%) tax on the excess $1,000.

Deductibility of IRA Contributions

Contributions to a traditional IRA can be deducted if neither spouse is covered by a retirement plan at work. However, these contributions may be limited if either spouse is covered by a retirement plan at work and their income exceeds certain threshold levels. When a couple files a joint return, the deduction is limited to the lesser of the following:

- $7,000 (or $8,000 if the spouse with the lower compensation is age 50 or older); or
- The total compensation in the couple's gross income, reduced by all of the following:
  - The IRA deduction of the spouse with the greater compensation
  - Any designated nondeductible contribution for the spouse with the greater compensation
  - Any contributions for a Roth IRA for the spouse with the greater compensation

28

As just noted, the deduction that can be taken for contributions to a traditional IRA depends on whether there was any coverage during the year by an employer retirement plan. When this is the case, the deduction may be reduced or eliminated. The deduction begins to decline when a person's income rises above a designated threshold amount, and is cancelled when it attains a higher threshold amount. The following table contains the basic rules for the amount of the deduction that can be taken.

Deductibility of Traditional IRA Contributions (Coverage by Retirement Plan)

Filing Status	Modified Adjusted Gross Income	Deduction Status
Single or head of household	$79,000 or less	Full deduction
	$79,001 to $89,000	Partial deduction
	$89,000+	No deduction
Married filing jointly	$126,000 or less	Full deduction
	$126,001 to $146,000	Partial deduction
	$146,000+	No deduction
Married filing separately	Less than $10,000	Partial deduction
	$10,000+	No deduction

EXAMPLE

Florence is 31 years old and single. She was covered by her retirement plan at work during the current year. Her modified AGI for the year is $90,000. Florence makes a $7,000 contribution to her traditional IRA for the year. Because she is covered by an employer retirement plan and her modified adjusted gross income exceeds the $89,000 threshold, she cannot deduct the contribution. Instead, it is classified as a nondeductible contribution.

All nondeductible contributions must be reported on Form 8606, *Nondeductible IRAs*. If these contributions are not reported on the form, then all distributions from the IRA will be taxed.

The following additional items pertain to deductibility:

- Contributions made to a Roth IRA are not deductible.
- Trustee's administrative fees that are billed separately in relation to an IRA are not deductible.
- Broker's commissions are considered part of an IRA contribution, and so are deductible.

Investment Options Not Allowed

It is not allowable to invest IRA funds in life insurance or collectibles. Examples of collectibles are alcoholic beverages, antiques, artwork, coins, metals, rugs, stamps, and certain other types of tangible personal property. An IRA trustee can impose additional restrictions on the types of allowable investments; for example, many trustees do not allow real estate investments, due to the administrative effort associated with them.

> **Note:** Though investments in metals are not allowed, it is permissible to invest in one, one-half, one-quarter, or one-tenth ounce U. S. gold coins, or one-ounce silver coins minted by the Treasury Department.

If a traditional IRA is used to invest in collectibles, the amount invested is considered to have been distributed to the account owner or beneficiary, which may trigger an early distribution tax.

Prohibited Transactions

The tax law prohibits an account owner or beneficiary from using an IRA in certain ways. These prohibited transactions are as follows:

- You cannot borrow money from an IRA. This is considered a distribution.
- You cannot sell property to an IRA.
- You cannot use an IRA as security on a loan. The amount used as security is considered a distribution.
- You cannot purchase property for personal use with IRA funds.

If an account owner or beneficiary engages in any of these prohibited transactions, the account stops being an IRA as of the first day of the year in which the prohibited activity occurred. This means that the account is treated as distributing all of its assets at their fair market values on the first day of the year. This will result in a taxable gain if the total of those values is more than the recipient's basis in the IRA. The distribution may also be subject to additional taxes and penalties.

Rollover Options

It might be useful to shift the balance in another investment vehicle into an IRA, or to shift funds out of an IRA and into a different investment vehicle. We discuss these concepts in the following paragraphs.

It is usually possible to roll over the balance in a workplace retirement account to an IRA. The only situations in which this is not allowed are as follows:

- A distribution that is one of a series of substantially equal payments
- Distributions of excess contributions and related earnings
- Distributions paid for accident, health or life insurance
- Dividends on employer securities
- Hardship distributions
- Loans classified as deemed distributions
- Required minimum distributions

- S corporation allocations treated as deemed distributions
- Withdrawals electing out of automatic contribution arrangements

Conversely, it is possible to roll over the balance in an IRA to a qualified retirement plan (such as a 401(k) plan) if the receiving plan allows it to accept such a rollover.

A distribution from a retirement plan that is to be rolled over into an IRA must be completed by the 60th day following the day on which the distribution was received. After that period, amounts not rolled over do not qualify for tax-free rollover treatment; instead, they are treated as a taxable distribution, and are taxable in the year distributed.

A traditional IRA can be converted to a Roth IRA by receiving a distribution from the IRA and contributing it to a Roth IRA within 60 days. Alternatively, the trustee holding the IRA can be instructed to transfer the funds directly to the trustee of the Roth IRA account. This conversion results in taxation of any untaxed amounts in the traditional IRA.

It is also possible to roll over the balance from one traditional IRA into another traditional IRA, as long as the funds are reinvested in the receiving IRA within 60 days. The rollover is only tax-free if the property being contributed to the receiving IRA is the same property received from the distributing IRA. A further rule is that a person can only make one rollover from an IRA to another IRA in any one-year period. However, there is no such limitation on trustee-to-trustee transfers. Also, there is no limitation on rollovers from traditional IRAs to Roth IRAs.

Tip: If an eligible rollover distribution is paid directly to you, the payer must withhold 20% of it, even if you plan to roll it over into a traditional IRA. This can be avoided by taking the direct rollover option, where the funds are sent directly to a traditional IRA.

Allowable Distributions

It is entirely allowable to take distributions from an IRA at any time, and there is no need to show hardship in order to do so. When a distribution is taken, the amount will appear in the account owner's taxable income. Depending on the circumstances, these distributions may be subject to an early distribution penalty, as described in the next section.

Early Distribution Penalties

Though a traditional IRA is designed to confer tax advantages on an account owner, these advantages can be more than offset by additional taxes and penalties if account usage rules are not followed. In particular, if a distribution is taken before an account owner is 59½ years old, it may be subject to a 10% additional tax. However, there are several exceptions that can be used to avoid the 10% tax, which are as follows:

- The recipient has unreimbursed medical expenses that are more than 7.5% of his or her adjusted gross income.
- The distributions made are not more than the cost of one's medical insurance, due to a period of unemployment.
- The recipient is totally and permanently disabled.
- The recipient is the beneficiary of an account owner who dies before reaching age 59½.
- The recipient is receiving distributions in the form of an annuity, as long as there is at least one distribution per year.
- The distributions do not exceed the amount of one's qualified higher education expenses. These expenses can be for the recipient or a spouse, children or grandchildren, and must be for tuition, fees, books, supplies, and equipment related to educational activities.
- The distributions are being used to acquire or build a first home, and do not exceed $10,000.
- The distribution is a qualified reservist distribution, where the recipient was called to active duty for a period of more than 179 days.
- The distribution is a qualified birth or adoption distribution, if made during the one-year period beginning on the date of birth or adoption, and for an amount not to exceed $5,000.

These exceptions also apply to distributions from a Roth IRA account.

EXAMPLE

Andrea is 10 years old. She receives a $1,500 distribution from her traditional IRA account. She does not qualify for any of the exceptions to the 10% additional tax, so the $4,500 is classified as an early distribution. Andrea must include the $4,500 in her gross income in the year in which the distribution was made, paying income tax on this amount. She must also pay an additional $450 tax (calculated as $4,500 distribution × 10% additional tax).

Further, a distribution taken from a SIMPLE IRA within the first two years of participation will be subject to an additional 25% tax.

Taxability of IRA Interest

The interest earned on funds stored in an IRA are not taxed in the year earned. Instead, the tax on this interest is deferred until a distribution is made from the account. Therefore, this interest is not reported to the IRS as tax-exempt interest.

Required Minimum Distributions

A minimum withdrawal is required for a traditional IRA, SIMPLE IRA and SEP IRA by April 1 of the year following the calendar years in which the account owner reaches age 73. This age is reduced to 70½ years for those born before July 1, 1949. The basic rules associated with these withdrawals are as follows:

- It is allowable to withdraw more than the minimum required amount.
- There is no exception from the required minimum withdrawals for those who are still working.
- Withdrawals must be included in taxable income except for any funds that had already been taxed, or which can be received tax-free. No withdrawal is required from a Roth IRA account until the death of the owner, since the funds placed in the account were already taxed.
- Subsequent withdrawals must be made by December 31 of each year. For the first year following the year when an account owner reaches the triggering age a distribution is required by April 1, followed by another withdrawal by December 31.

EXAMPLE

Emily reaches age 73 on September 15, 2024. She must receive her 2024 required minimum distribution by April 1, 2025, based on her 2024 year-end balance. Emily must receive her 2025 required minimum distribution by December 31, 2025, based on her 2025 year-end balance.

The required minimum distribution in each year is the account balance at the end of the immediately preceding calendar year, divided by the distribution period stated on the IRS's Uniform Lifetime Table for the account owner's age. This table is used for unmarried account owners, married owners whose spouses are not more than 10 years younger, and married owners whose spouses are not the sole beneficiaries of their IRAs. Distributions reduce the account balance in the year they are made. Thus, a distribution for 2024 made after December 31 of 2025 reduces the account balance for 2025, not 2024. The Uniform Lifetime Table appears in the following exhibit. In deciding whether to use the table, marital status is determined as of January 1 of each year; any divorce or death is disregarded until the following year.

Uniform Lifetime Table

Age	Distribution Period	Age	Distribution Period
72	27.4	95	8.9
73	26.5	96	8.4
74	25.5	97	7.8
75	24.6	98	7.3
76	23.7	99	6.8
77	22.9	100	6.4
78	22.0	101	6.0
79	21.1	102	5.6
80	20.2	103	5.2
81	19.4	104	4.9
82	18.5	105	4.6
83	17.7	106	4.3
84	16.8	107	4.1
85	16.0	108	3.9
86	15.2	109	3.7
87	14.4	110	3.5
88	13.7	111	3.4
89	12.9	112	3.3
90	12.2	113	3.1
91	11.5	114	3.0
92	10.8	115	2.9
93	10.1	116	1.8
94	9.5	117+	2.7

EXAMPLE

Francis owns a traditional IRA. His account balance at the end of 2024 was $200,000. His sole beneficiary is his spouse, who is two years younger. Francis will be 80 years old in 2025. According to the Uniform Lifetime Table, his distribution period is 20.2. Therefore, his required distribution amount is $9,901 (calculated as $200,000 ÷ 20.2).

If a beneficiary is the account owner's surviving spouse and sole designated beneficiary, then this person will also use the Uniform Lifetime Table to calculate required minimum distributions. However, if the account owner had not yet reached age 73 when he or she died, and the beneficiary elected not to be treated as the owner of the

IRA, then the beneficiary does not have to take any distributions until the year in which the account owner would have reached age 73.

Table I (Single Life Expectancy) is used by beneficiaries who are not the spouse of the account owner, while Table II (Joint Life and Last Survivor Expectancy) is intended for owners whose spouses are more than 10 years younger, and are the account owner's sole beneficiaries. Table I appears in the following exhibit.

Table I, Single Life Expectancy (for use by beneficiaries)

Age	Life Expectancy	Age	Life Expectancy	Age	Life Expectancy	Age	Life Expectancy
0	84.6	28	57.3	56	30.6	84	8.7
1	83.7	29	56.3	57	29.8	85	8.1
2	82.8	30	55.3	58	28.9	86	7.6
3	81.8	31	54.4	59	28.0	87	7.1
4	80.8	32	53.4	60	27.1	88	6.6
5	79.8	33	52.5	61	26.2	89	6.1
6	78.8	34	51.5	62	25.4	90	5.7
7	77.9	35	50.5	63	24.5	91	5.3
8	76.9	36	49.6	64	23.7	92	4.9
9	75.9	37	48.6	65	22.9	93	4.6
10	74.9	38	47.7	66	22.0	94	4.3
11	73.9	39	46.7	67	21.2	95	4.0
12	72.9	40	45.7	68	20.4	96	3.7
13	71.9	41	44.8	69	19.6	97	3.4
14	70.9	42	43.8	70	18.8	98	3.2
15	69.9	43	42.9	71	18.0	99	3.0
16	69.0	44	41.9	72	17.2	100	2.8
17	68.0	45	41.0	73	16.4	101	2.6
18	67.0	46	40.0	74	15.6	102	2.5
19	66.0	47	39.0	75	14.8	103	2.3
20	65.0	48	38.1	76	14.1	104	2.2
21	64.1	49	37.1	77	13.3	105	2.1
22	63.1	50	36.2	78	12.6	106	2.1
23	62.1	51	35.3	79	11.9	107	2.1
24	61.1	52	34.3	80	11.2	108	2.0
25	60.2	53	33.4	81	10.5	109	2.0
26	59.2	54	32.5	82	9.9	110	2.0
27	58.2	55	31.6	83	9.3	111+	2.0

EXAMPLE

Mary is the surviving spouse and the sole designated beneficiary. Her husband, Jonathan, would have been 73 years old in 2024, so distributions will begin in 2024. Mary becomes 67 years old in 2024. She uses Table I, Single Life Expectancy, to determine her distribution period, which is 21.2.

Note: If an account owner receives more than the required minimum distribution in any given year, the excess payment cannot be applied as a credit when determining the required minimum distributions for subsequent years.

The annual required minimum distribution can be taken in a series of installment payments over the course of the year, as long as the total distribution amount at least equals the minimum requirement.

There are substantial penalties for not taking required minimum distributions. An account owner may be charged a 50% excise tax on the amount not distributed as required. You can apply for a waiver from this tax when a distribution shortfall was due to an error and you are taking steps to remedy the situation.

Summary

An IRA can be quite a useful way to avoid the recognition of income until your retirement. However, an IRA must be used within the rules, or else taxes and penalties could offset or even exceed this benefit. In particular, you should be cognizant of the income levels at which contributions are no longer deductible, avoid early distributions, and be sure to take the required minimum distribution. In particular, the required minimum distribution *must* be observed, or else you could be hit with a 50% excise tax.

Chapter 4
Investing in Stocks

Introduction

In this chapter, we cover the essentials of investing in stocks, including how to conduct research, types of investing strategies, and investing best practices. We also cover the business activities and types of information that can move stock prices. The advice provided in this chapter is critical for the development of a coherent long-term strategy for investing in stocks.

How Businesses Raise Money

Before we discuss investing in stocks, it may be worthwhile to briefly discuss how businesses raise money. An organization may sometimes need extra cash to expand its operations, invest in new products, or build its working capital in order to fund more inventory and receivables. The best fundraising route for a small business is through a loan from the local bank, but the options expand considerably for larger firms. One option is to sell bonds to investors. A bond is classified as debt, since the issuer promises to repay the bond on its maturity date, and also makes regular interest payments to investors. Companies are more likely to issue bonds when the market interest rate is low, and especially when the share price is low (meaning that the owners would have to give up a large ownership interest in the company in order to raise a sufficient amount of money).

The other fundraising option is to sell shares in the business. Once sold to investors, these shares can be traded on a stock exchange, allowing investors to readily liquidate their investments. An issuer is not required to buy back shares, though some companies occasionally do so. Instead, investors make money from periodic dividend payments, as well as from any appreciation in the price of the shares on the stock market. A share issuance is a good choice for a rapidly growing company that needs a large amount of funding, and does not have the cash flow to buy back bonds from investors. It is also a good idea when the stock market is peaking, or when market interest rates are so high that bond financing would be too expensive. The primary downside to selling shares to the public is the onerous reporting requirements associated with doing so, which can be quite burdensome – especially for smaller businesses that do not have the financial resources to pay for these activities.

How Businesses Add Value

When companies sell shares to the public, their investors want to experience some price appreciation in their holdings. This happens when demand for those shares increases, which is triggered by either reporting higher profits or the anticipation of higher profits in the future. Therefore, to meet shareholder demand for higher share prices, a business may engage in any (or all) of the following activities:

- *Add markets.* One of the easier ways to increase profits is to increase the number of markets in which a company's goods are sold. For example, a company that manufactures furniture could begin by selling its products in just one state, and then within the surrounding states, then nationwide, and then internationally. However, these expansions can increase the complexity of operating the business, and may require the use of partners to assist in selling, which tends to reduce profits. In addition, products may require some modification to be successful in foreign markets, which can also impact profits.
- *Build a brand.* A business can invest heavily in advertising and product quality in order to increase brand recognition. This can allow a business to increase its prices, though the brand-building exercise does not always succeed, and must be reinforced over time with additional expenditures.
- *Control costs.* Any business needs to maintain tight control over its cost structure. This must be done carefully, so that cost reductions do not impact the quality of a company's products. Cost control can be something of a minefield for businesses that are also building brand recognition, since branding requires major expenditures, and mandates that a high level of product quality be maintained.
- *Enter adjacent markets.* If a company's current market niche has been largely exploited, then a logical next step is to enter adjacent markets where it can take advantage of its existing expertise. For example, a garden products company could expand into lawn care, while a manufacturer of automobiles could expand into the production of trucks. This approach can be difficult, since some additional expertise must be acquired when entering adjacent markets.
- *Invest in new product development.* When the investment community sees that a business is rolling out new products that can increase its sales and profits, demand for its shares will increase. However, this is not an easy path to follow. The business must be able to convert its research efforts into workable products that beat the offerings of competitors, and without excessively cannibalizing sales of the firm's existing products. In short, new product development must be carefully managed.
- *Pursue niches.* A potentially very profitable approach is to find underserved niches in the market and fill the needs of those customers. This may involve a significant repositioning of the company, perhaps with specially-designed products, different customer service, and so forth. If done successfully, customers may be willing to pay higher prices for the firm's goods and services.

The job of the investor, or the investor's advisors, is to monitor how well companies are pursuing these strategies, and to invest in those whose efforts appear most likely to generate outsized profits. It also means selling off the shares of those entities whose strategies appear to be failing or at least underperforming. This is very much a forward-looking effort, since other investors are also engaged in this research, and their collective opinion of the prospects of a business is reflected in the current market price.

Characteristics of Stocks

A *stock* is a security that represents the ownership of a fraction of a corporation. This ownership interest entitles the owner to a proportion of the firm's assets and profits. Units of stock are called *shares*. Stock ownership is a good way for investors to share in the wealth generated by businesses, since the historical rate of return on these investments has exceeded the rate of inflation.

There are two ways in which an investor can earn a return on stock holdings. One is through dividend payments. A *dividend* is a payment to shareholders of a portion of a corporation's earnings. The amount to be paid is decided by the organization's board of directors. The payment is nearly always in cash, but can also take the form of property or additional shares of stock. Larger companies are more likely to pay dividends, because they have a stable stream of income from which to make payments. Smaller, rapidly-growing businesses need every penny they can get to fund their growth, and so are much less likely to pay dividends.

The other way for investors to earn a return is via increases in the price of their stock holdings. When this happens and investors want to pocket the proceeds, they sell the shares on a stock exchange, thereby converting the shares into cash. It is also entirely possible that share prices will decline, in which case selling them will result in a loss for an investor.

The Stock Market

When we refer to the *stock market*, we are talking about the collection of exchanges at which the shares of publicly-traded companies are bought and sold. These transactions are conducted through physical or electronic exchanges, or through the over-the-counter market (which operates under different rules). There are many stock exchanges, including the New York Stock Exchange, the NASDAQ, and the Tokyo Stock Exchange.

In brief, stock exchanges provide a secure and (very) regulated environment in which to buy and sell financial instruments, with minimal operational risk. An exchange can act is a primary market, where a company conducts an initial public offering, selling its shares for the first time to investors. Or (and more commonly), it acts as a secondary exchange, where investors buy and sell shares amongst themselves. Issuing companies directly benefit from the cash received from primary markets, while their investors benefit from the secondary exchange role. In either role, a stock exchange facilitates transactions, and is paid a fee for doing so.

Stock exchanges operating within the United States are monitored by the Securities and Exchange Commission (SEC). The SEC also protects the investing public by promoting the full disclosure of financial information, as well as by investigating cases of financial fraud. In addition, the SEC specifies the reporting requirements of all publicly-held entities within the country, and makes their filings available to the general public on its website.

Investors commonly track the overall trend of stock valuations within the stock market with one or more stock indexes. A *stock index* is a group of shares that are used to give an indication of the stock market as a whole or a subset of it. A good index to use that reasonably represents the performance of the stock market as a whole is the Standard & Poor's 500 Index. It contains 500 companies based in the United States, which represent about 80% of the total value of the stock market. A more comprehensive index is the Wilshire 5000, which includes all publicly-traded companies with headquarters in the United States. The NASDAQ Composite Index is derived from more than 3,000 stocks that are listed on the NASDAQ stock exchange. Since the NASDAQ lists the stocks of a disproportionate share of technology companies, it tends to be more representative of the performance of that sector.

Perhaps the most commonly-cited index is the Dow Jones Industrial Average (DJIA), which includes the stocks of 30 large companies that are based in the United States. The DJIA represents about 25% of the value of the stock market. However, since the DJIA only contains the stocks of very large companies, it does not necessarily represent investor opinions regarding the rest of the market.

The main use of stock indexes is to give you a quick view of the direction in which the market is heading, which is a gauge of investor sentiment. These indexes can also be used to compare the performance of a single stock to a representation of the market as a whole, to see if it is underperforming or overperforming.

Market Moving Events

Financial markets tend to be quite efficient, because there are many buyers and sellers, and they all have access to approximately the same information. Consequently, only new information that the investment community has not yet seen should impact the markets to a significant extent. Market prices move a lot, so clearly a great deal of information is constantly impacting the markets. What types of information have the most immediate impact on the market? Here are some pointers:

- *Earnings reports*. Publicly-held companies are required to issue their financial results once a quarter, and their annual results following the end of each fiscal year. In addition, they may hold earnings calls, which are conference calls in which they clarify the information presented in their financial statements. When several companies in an industry sector report unusually high or low earnings, this is a signal to investors that the economy is changing. For example, a cluster of low earnings reports is a strong signal that the economy is cresting, and may be about to head into a recession.
- *Economic indicators*. An *economic indicator* is economic data used to interpret the current or future state of the economy. Investors are especially interested in *leading indicators*, which predict future economic activity levels. Examples of leading indicators are the number of new building permits, surveys of consumer sentiment, and new orders for manufacturers. The release of leading indicators to the public can definitely deliver a jolt to the financial markets – in either direction.
- *Interest rates*. The stock market goes up when interest rates decline, and reverses direction when interest rates increase. The reason is that heightened interest rates increase borrowing costs, which tends to contract economic

activity, driving down profits. Also, when interest rates increase, investor money tends to shift out of the stock market and into bonds and other debt instruments. Conversely, when interest rates are low, investors shift their money out of bonds and back into the stock market, which drives up prices.

- *Political changes.* The markets will react when a different political party or politician takes over a country. This represents a change in continuity, which can alter the underlying economics of a country. For example, when a social-ist-leaning government is replaced by a free-market government, the financial markets are likely to jump up, on the expectation that taxes and trade barriers will be lowered, resulting in more corporate profits.
- *Supply and demand.* Changes in supply and demand can definitely impact the financial markets. For example, when there is a constriction in the supply of key goods, such as computer chips, this constricts the sales of downstream products that use computer chips, resulting in reduced sales and profits. Con-versely, the opening of a major new computer chip factory would tend to have the reverse impact, since it tends to expand the sales of downstream products.
- *Wars.* Markets tend to drop when a war starts, because borders are closed, making it more difficult to transport goods across borders. A minor war in a distant region is unlikely to have much of an impact, but a major one may send the markets into a tail spin. These conflicts will have varying impacts on individual companies, however. For example, a war in Ethiopia would tank the stocks of any coffee plantations in the area whose production will be im-pacted, but will raise the stock prices of competitors located elsewhere, which will benefit from the reduced level of coffee supply.

Investing Strategies

The traditional investing strategies have been the growth, value, and income ap-proaches, which are described first in the following bullet points. We follow those strategies with a number of more specialized techniques, such as ones relating to ex-pected or rumored merger activity. Also, high frequency trading comprises a large part of all trades in a company's securities, though it is not based on a long-term in-vestment strategy. The most common approaches to investing are as follows:

- *Growth strategy.* Some investors buy shares of companies in their early stages of development, on the assumption that these businesses will ramp up quickly and experience high rates of revenue growth. They then sell their shares once a company's fundamentals appear to be maturing, with lower growth rates and a steady proportion of market share. These investors are particularly fo-cused on the rate of growth of a company's revenues and earnings per share, as well as the speed with which they are growing in comparison to the rest of the industry. Once a business reports a slower rate of growth, expect these types of investors to sell out, which may put downward pressure on the stock price.

- *Value strategy.* Some investors will only buy stock when it is trading at multiples notably lower than those of the industry at large. They will hold the shares until such time as they believe the shares have returned to the industry average, and then sell the shares. These investors are most interested in the ratio of a company's share price to its book value, which they will compare to the same ratio for other companies in the same industry. In addition, they delve into the basic earnings fundamentals of a business, to ensure that the current low valuation is not caused by financial issues that could derail their investment. Also, they are more likely to buy a company's shares shortly after it declares a profit warning, since the warning probably triggers a price decline. An interesting side effect of having value investors is that their purchasing activities tend to keep a share price from dropping too low, while their planned selling tends to keep share prices from rising too high. Thus, value investors tend to have a moderating influence on stock price volatility.

- *Income strategy.* Some investors are only concerned with the dividend payments they receive from their investments. The issuance of a continuing series of dividends will attract this group of investors, and they will leave immediately if a company reduces, delays, or eliminates its dividend. These investors are most interested in an uninterrupted history of dividends, a continuing increase in the dividend amount paid per share, and enough information about the fundamentals of the business to gain assurance that the dividend will not be reduced.

- *Growth at a reasonable price.* Some investors are positioned midway between the growth and value strategies. They buy shares when the current market valuation of a business appears inordinately low, but only in conjunction with a reasonable prospect for future growth. They will still sell their shares when a company's valuation has reached a certain point in relation to the industry average, but may also retain their holdings somewhat longer if the prospect of additional revenue growth appears to warrant the risk of retention.

- *High frequency trading.* The majority of all securities trades are now initiated by entities that engage in high frequency trading. These firms are essentially market makers, since they buy shares from sellers at the bid price, and then sell the shares to other investors at the offer price a few moments later, earning a fraction of a cent per share. This can be called an investing strategy, since the traders are buying and selling – they are just not holding shares for very long. Clearly, these investors have no interest in the financial condition of a company whose shares they are trading.

- *Technical analysis strategy.* Some investors are extremely active with their investments, closely tracking the historical behavior of stock prices and using this information to estimate where stock prices will be in the very near future. One of the more popular versions of technical analysis is momentum investing, which is the theory that securities that have done well in the recent past will continue to do so in the near future. These investors have only a moderate interest in a company's fundamentals, since they are moving in and out of investment positions on a continual basis.

- *Merger arbitrage strategy*. Investors buy the shares of companies that they believe will be acquired, and profit from the eventual (and presumably higher) price at which acquisitions are completed. This strategy can result in massive surges and declines in stock volume as acquisition rumors ebb and flow.
- *Roll up strategy*. There are rare cases where a company is unusually good at acquiring and wringing excellent results out of other businesses. Investors look for a continuing history of acquisitions that routinely result in accretive increases in earnings. They buy shares in acquiring businesses that show accretive earnings, in hopes that the gradual accumulation of purchasing power and other advantages by the acquirer will yield outsized earnings, and therefore sharp increases in the stock price.
- *Theme investment strategy*. Some investors prefer to obtain deep knowledge about a particular industry or commodity, and only invest in those areas. For example, an investor may choose to invest solely in the automobile manufacturing market. As another example, an investor may be an expert on the impact of changes in the price of copper on many industries, and chooses investments based on those impacts. These investors are less concerned with the fundamental profitability of a specific business; instead, they tend to buy or sell the shares of clusters of similar companies.

Note the different types of information that growth and value investors use. Growth investors are most concerned with the information appearing on a company's income statement, while value investors are more concerned with the book value information appearing on the balance sheet. A technical investor or a theme investor has less interest in either information source.

The following bullet points do not describe additional investment strategies; instead, they address the circumstances under which a person comes into the ownership of company shares. These sometimes inadvertent investors may have no real strategy for what to do with the stock. Where possible, we have noted their possible reactions to stock ownership. The "strategies" are:

- *Company employees*. Some people own shares in a business simply because they happen to be employees of the company. The company may have issued shares to them as part of an initial public offering, or for other reasons. These shares are likely to be initially restricted, with a waiting period and other requirements being imposed before they can be sold. Not all employees are financially sophisticated, and their shareholdings may also be extremely small. For both reasons, there tends to not be much activity in these shares. If anything, company employees tend to forget that they even *own* the shares. If employees do remember their shareholdings, they are more likely to retain them out of loyalty to the company.
- *Inheritance*. An individual may inherit shares. If so, there are two possible outcomes. One is that the recipient is barely aware of the shares (usually when the shareholding is quite minor), in which case the shares are unlikely to be traded. The other outcome is that the recipient is financially sophisticated, and

will immediately roll the shares into his or her portfolio; if the shares do not match the person's investment strategy, they will be sold.

- *Stock options*. Members of the management team, and sometimes other employees that a business wants to retain will be issued stock options, under which they have the option to purchase company shares at a certain price within a specific date range. Any shares purchased under a stock option plan are likely to be restricted, and so will not be traded for some time. However, the recipients of shares purchased under stock option plans will face a tax burden from their earnings, and so will likely sell at least some of these shares as soon as possible in order to generate enough cash to pay their tax obligations. Thus, an exercised stock option will likely lead to the sale of a portion of the related shares as soon as they become unrestricted.

- *Stock purchase plans*. Some companies offer stock purchase plans to their employees, under which the employees can buy shares through ongoing payroll deductions, and usually at a discount to the market price. Participants in stock purchase plans tend to be somewhat more financially sophisticated, and so will be more likely to sell their shares at the right price.

This last group of points indicates that the circumstances under which shareholders come by their shares can have an impact on their propensity to hold or sell the shares.

Mutual Funds

Thus far, we have assumed that investors want to purchase the shares of particular companies. What if this is not the case? You might not want to spend the time required to research companies. If so, a mutual fund might be a better approach to investing. A *mutual fund* is a type of financial vehicle that is made up of a pool of money obtained from a large number of investors; its goal is to invest the money in a variety of securities, as stated in its prospectus. The money is invested by a group of professional money managers. Any gains or losses are allocated proportionally among the investors. Investing in a mutual fund is a good way to go for investors that do not have enough time to conduct their own investment research. A further advantage is that the fund's holdings can be diversified across many assets, thereby reducing the likelihood of suffering significant losses. The main downside to these funds is that the fund manager decides when to sell assets, which can result in taxable distributions at inopportune moments.

A variation on the mutual fund concept is the *exchange-traded fund* (ETF), which invests in a particular index, industry, or commodity. It is easy to invest in an ETF, since it is traded on a stock exchange. The operating expenses of an ETF that follows an index are especially low, since there are no investment decisions to be made.

Hedge Funds

A *hedge fund* pools the money of contributing investors and tries to achieve above-market returns through a wide variety of investment strategies. Larger investors are attracted to the higher returns advertised by hedge funds, though actual returns are not necessarily better than the average market rate of return. Hedge funds do not necessarily subscribe to a particular investment philosophy, so they can roam the investment landscape, looking for anomalies of all types to take advantage of. However, they usually develop investment strategies that are designed to generate gains, irrespective of movements in the stock market, either up or down.

Hedge funds typically do not accept small investments, with minimum contributions starting as high as $1 million. Hedge fund managers are compensated with a percentage of the total assets in the investment pool, as well as a percentage of all profits generated. For example, a fund manager could take 2% of all capital under management, as well as 20% of all profits earned.

Hedge fund investment strategies may include the following options:

- *Leverage strategy*. There may be a considerable quantity of leverage (that is, investing borrowed funds) to achieve outsized returns on a relatively small capital base. This presents the risk that losses on leveraged funds can be outsized, triggering massive losses for investors.
- *Short sales strategy*. Hedge funds may borrow shares and sell them, in the expectation that the price of a security will drop, after which they buy the securities on the open market and return the borrowed securities. This is a very risky strategy, since a share price increase can introduce potentially unlimited losses for investors.
- *Derivatives strategy*. Investments are made in any number of derivatives, which can pay off based on a vast number of possible underlying indices or other measures.

Because of the enhanced use of leverage, as well as other speculative strategies, there is a much higher probability of loss in a hedge fund than would be the case in a more traditional investment fund that only invests in the securities of well-established companies. The level of potential loss is accentuated by the common requirement that investments cannot be withdrawn from a hedge fund for a period of at least one year. This requirement is needed because some hedge fund investments cannot be easily liquidated to meet a cash withdrawal demand by an investor. The requirement also allows a hedge fund manager to employ longer-term investment strategies.

Hedge funds avoid oversight by the Securities and Exchange Commission (SEC) by only allowing investments by large institutions and accredited investors (individuals with a large net worth or income). This means that hedge funds do not have to report as much information to their investors or the SEC.

Note: The term "hedge" in the name "hedge fund" is a misnomer, since it seems to imply that a fund attempts to mitigate its risk. This term comes from the early days of hedge funds, when funds attempted to reduce the risk of securities price declines in a bear market by shorting securities. Nowadays, the pursuit of outsized returns is the primary goal, and that cannot usually be achieved while risk is also being hedged.

A Word on Speculative Bubbles

It is all too easy for investors to be sucked into *speculative bubbles*, which are spikes in asset values that are fueled by irrational speculative activity that is not supported by the fundamentals. These situations arise when someone who bought in at a low price promotes the idea that a security is bound to increase in value, which in turn brings in more investors who also promote it, in hopes of a further rise in value. This "piling on" effect does indeed keep raising the price, but eventually there are no more new investors willing to buy, at which point demand falls, triggering a steep decline in the price – and many investor losses.

There are a few general rules to follow to avoid speculative bubbles. First, always look at the fundamentals. For example, if the price/earnings ratio (see the Investing Metrics chapter) has been trending up steeply, then it is already too late to buy a security. Or, if the underlying business is not generating positive cash flow, then there is no basis for a high stock price valuation. Second, look at the metrics being cited. If someone has developed a new investing metric to justify a high valuation, such as a revenue to stock price multiple instead of the usual price/earnings ratio, then be very suspicious. Third, if short sellers are betting heavily against the company, there is probably a good reason for it. Short sellers dig through a company's financials for signs of problems, and will sell short in the expectation of a future drop in the stock price.

When it is apparent that a speculative bubble is building, this is a good time to park your excess cash in a money market account and wait for the bubble to burst. When stock prices have dropped in the aftermath of the crash, swoop in with your excess funds and buy shares at their new "value" prices.

> **Tip:** As the global population continues to expand into every corner of the globe, the amount of infrastructure required to support it must also expand – which means that a hiccup anywhere in the system can cause major problems for the world economy at any time. That being the case, it is likely that the next hiccup – whatever it is – is probably only a few years away. Therefore, maintain a good reserve of cash for the inevitable stock market downturns associated with these events, and get ready to buy on the downturn.

Penny Stock Concerns

A variation on the speculative bubble to guard against is anyone pushing penny stocks. A *penny stock* refers to a small company's stock that trades for less than $5 per share, and which trades over-the-counter, rather than through a stock exchange. These stocks trade at such low volumes that it is easy to manipulate their share prices. For example, a brokerage could assign one of these penny stocks to its sales staff, who call likely prospects to drum up interest in it. They typically tout the stock as being about to take off in price, which means that buying it right now at a bargain price of $___ will assure gargantuan profits down the road. The usual outcome is that the brokerage sells the stock at an inflated price, pockets a large profit, and then leaves the investors to suffer losses as the stock price declines back to where it was before the brokerage got involved. In short, when someone calls you with such a sales pitch, hang up. The same advice applies to any other form of investment-related communication.

How to Judge Your Investing Performance

All too many investors want to see immediate improvements in the value of their stock portfolios. If they do not see increases within a few months – or even weeks – then they sell their holdings and try something else. This is most unwise, since the valuation of your portfolio will fluctuate over an extended period of time. For example, there may be two or three years of moderately steady increases, followed by a sharp decline, followed by a few years of variable outcomes. How you judge the performance of the portfolio depends on when you acquired stocks during this series of events. A better approach is to monitor portfolio performance over a much longer period of time, such as five to 10 years. By doing so, you will be less inclined to continually swap out stocks, which in turn minimizes sales commissions. A further advantage is that holding stocks for longer periods of time qualifies any gains to be taxed at the much lower long-term capital gains rate. Conversely, if you constantly buy and sell shares, then any gains on a stock held for less than one year would be taxed at the higher short-term rate. A final advantage of only measuring your performance over the long term is that it ensures that you have money invested in the stock market at all times – which positions your money perfectly to benefit from unexpected jumps in stock prices. If you had instead been jumping in and out of the market, there is a good chance that you would miss one of the run-ups in price.

In short, stocks are intended to be long-term investments, so only measure their performance over the long term. Any shorter investment interval can result in adverse investing behavior that can reduce your return on investment.

Best Practices for Investing in Stocks

As we noted earlier in the Investing Strategies section, there are many approaches to investing. No matter which one you follow, these best practices will enhance your ability to earn a solid return on investment:

- *Avoid market timing.* It is impossible to predict when the market will rise or fall, so don't try to time your stock purchases for the absolute low point of the market. Instead, make purchases on a regular basis.
- *Avoid taxes.* Income taxes can whittle down your returns, so invest through a tax-advantaged retirement account first, and try to hold stocks for a sufficiently long time to qualify any resulting gains for long-term capital gains tax treatment.
- *Diversify your investments.* Always spread your money among a number of unrelated investments. This means investing in companies of different sizes, in different industries, and in different countries. Doing so insulates you from problems that may trigger valuation declines in specific market niches.

47

- *Minimize costs.* Minimize your trading fees by buying and holding stocks. Also, invest in funds where the management fees are low. Doing so can have a notably positive impact on your total investment return.
- *Use investment funds.* Outsource the investing work to a professional. You probably don't have the time required to dig into the fundamentals of every company you want to invest in, so don't try – leave it to someone who does it for a living.

Above all, be calm. Do not sell in the midst of a massive market downturn, or be lured into investing in a "hot" sector, or buy when it seems that everyone else is piling into the market. Instead of following the herd, just devise an investment plan that works for you, and follow it consistently. It is easier to do this if you are not constantly monitoring the state of your investments. Instead, an end-of-month peek at the numbers should be more than enough for the long-term investor.

Conducting Stock Research

There are many sources of information about stocks, some of which are freely available on the Internet. For example, a search on the Google Finance site for Wells Fargo reveals the following information (of which there is more information lower on the website page):

Google Finance Summary of Wells Fargo

Wells Fargo & Co

$70.69 ↑22.70% +13.08 1Y

Pre-market: $69.62 (↓1.51%) -1.07

Closed: Mar 31, 9:21:32 AM UTC-4 · USD · NYSE · Disclaimer

1D 5D 1M 6M YTD 1Y 5Y MAX

0.0% of your portfolio
Only you can see this

+ Add to portfolio

Stock   US listed security

US headquartered

PREVIOUS CLOSE	$70.69
YEAR RANGE	$50.15 – $81.50
MARKET CAP	230.81B USD
AVG VOLUME	16.96M
P/E RATIO	13.17
DIVIDEND YIELD	2.26%
PRIMARY EXCHANGE	NYSE

Compare to

Bank of America Corp	Citigroup Inc	JPMorgan Chase & Co	Morgan Stanley
$41.25	$70.33	$242.85	$115.33
BAC ↑9.94%	C ↑10.83%	JPM ↑22.07%	MS ↑23.31%

Or, for a different presentation of this information as of the same day, the following exhibit contains the presentation for Wells Fargo, as compiled by Yahoo Finance.

Yahoo Finance Summary of Wells Fargo

Wells Fargo & Company (WFC) ☆ Follow ⤴ Compare

70.18 -0.51 (-0.72%)
As of 9:32:11 AM EDT. Market Open.

| 1D | 5D | 1M | 6M | YTD | 1Y | 5Y | All | | | Key Events | ▲ Mountain ⌄ | ✐ Advanced Chart | ⚙ |

Previous Close	70.69	Day's Range	70.05 - 70.36	Market Cap (intraday)	229.182B	Earnings Date	Apr 11, 2025
Open	72.26	52 Week Range	50.15 - 81.50	Beta (5Y Monthly)	1.16	Forward Dividend & Yield	1.60 (2.26%)
Bid	69.71 x 1300	Volume	65,689	PE Ratio (TTM)	13.05	Ex-Dividend Date	Feb 7, 2025
Ask	69.90 x 800	Avg. Volume	16,067,362	EPS (TTM)	5.37	1y Target Est	83.10

Explanations for a selection of the data stated in the preceding two exhibits are noted in the following table.

Finance Summary Explanations

Data Item	Description
Previous Close	The prior day's final price of a security when the market officially closes for the day
Day Range	The lowest and highest prices at which a stock traded during the day
Market Cap	The value of all outstanding shares, calculated as the number of outstanding shares times the current market price per share
Volume	The number of shares traded in the current trading day
P/E Ratio	The price of the company's stock in relation to its reported earnings
Dividend Yield	The effective yield produced by the firm's dividends, which is the dividend divided by the stock price
Primary Exchange	The main stock exchange on which the company's stock is traded
52-Week Range	The lowest and highest prices at which a stock traded during the past year
EPS	The reported earnings of the business divided by the average amount of shares outstanding during the period
Ex-Dividend Date	The first date following the declaration of a dividend by a company; on this date, the purchaser of the firm's stock is not entitled to receive the next dividend payment

It can be useful to subscribe to one of the many services that provide more in-depth analyses of businesses, such as Morningstar and Value Line. These organizations employ analysts who usually specialize in just a single industry. Their commentaries on individual stocks can assist in forming an opinion about whether to make an investment or change an existing one.

Another excellent source of information is the website of the SEC, which is located at www.sec.gov. The SEC posts the public filings of all publicly-held company companies on this website. Once downloaded from the SEC website, you can review the financial statements of a business; a later chapter on the interpretation of financial statements may be of use in analyzing these statements.

The financial statements of a publicly-held company are contained within the Form 10-K, which is the annual report required by the SEC. The 10-K is extremely detailed and factual, and so is the main source of information for many investors. Companies must also issue the shorter Form 10-Q on a quarterly basis; it contains the firm's quarterly financial statements, along with somewhat less accompanying financial information than is contained within the 10-K.

The financial statements in a company's Form 10-K must be audited, which means that an outside audit firm has examined the firm's accounting records and inspected its assets. The audit firm's opinion regarding the financial statements is then included in the Form 10-K. The financial statements in a company's Form 10-Q only need to be reviewed by the auditors; this is a lesser examination that provides a reduced level of assurance regarding the firm's financial statements. For a review, the auditors must perform analytical procedures and make inquiries concerning the financial statements and accompanying footnote disclosures.

Note: Another option for finding stock recommendations is to access the quarterly Form 13F filings of prominent investment funds on the SEC website. These reports state their stock holdings. You can decide whether to copy their investments, or perhaps try a variation on them.

Summary

We have noted a variety of investing strategies in this chapter, along with how to collect more information to support whichever approach you prefer. Even more important are the concepts of developing a diverse portfolio and of investing over the long term. Though it is possible to win big from a single investment, a much more prudent approach is to spread your money among a range of unrelated investments, so that a loss on any one investment will have only a modest impact on your returns. And, be aware that the best returns only occur over the long term. This means sticking with your investments for years, rather than constantly churning your portfolio. These two principles make it much more likely that your investing activities will bear fruit.

Chapter 5
Investing in Lending Arrangements

Introduction

There are several types of lending arrangements in which investments can be made, such as savings accounts, certificates of deposit, and bonds. Under these arrangements, you essentially lend money to the recipient in exchange for what is usually a fixed payment – there is no upside potential for additional payments, nor is there any resulting ownership in the recipient entity. In this chapter, we cover the characteristics of lending arrangements and how to buy bonds.

Characteristics of Lending Arrangements

The main benefit of any lending arrangement is a steady stream of interest payments from the borrower. This is not a minor issue, since it can provide some income stability, especially when the bulk of your assets are parked in more volatile equity investments that may not make any periodic payments, and which might even decline in value over time. This level of stability and income makes lending arrangements a good choice for investors who need some ongoing income, and especially so when the prospect of investment volatility makes it difficult for them to sleep at night.

Balanced against these benefits is the lower return on lending arrangements, which can make it difficult to attain any net return after the negative effects of inflation are considered. Furthermore, investing in these instruments means that you are not using the money to invest in higher-return stocks or real estate, so the opportunity cost of lending arrangements can be substantial.

Lending Choices

The main lending choices are products offered by banks, money market funds, and bonds. In the following sub-sections, we cover all of these topics and pay particular attention to the different types of bonds and their features.

Banks

Banks offer both savings accounts and certificates of deposit. Savings accounts pay a minor interest rate and allow for immediate withdrawals, while certificates of deposit pay a somewhat higher rate, but in exchange for not being able to withdraw the cash early (or at least not without having to pay a fee). The interest paid by banks is usually quite low, because they must also pay for their operating costs – which can be substantial. A benefit of parking money in a bank is the $250,000 account insurance provided by the federal government. However, the interest rates offered are painfully low, so it can make sense to explore other options.

> **Tip:** The rates offered by online banks tend to be higher than the rates offered by traditional ones, because online banks have no retail branches, and therefore less overhead. If you decide to open a savings account with an online bank, investigate it beforehand to see if it has FDIC insurance coverage. To do so, search for the bank's name on the following website:
>
> https://banks.data.fdic.gov/bankfind-suite/bankfind

When deciding whether to invest your funds through a bank, conduct some analysis first. This means calling their customer service phone line to see how easy it is to reach an actual person. If it is not, then consider how difficult it will be to deal with the bank when you actually need it. Second, explore the available options for withdrawing cash. If cash withdrawals are made through an ATM, will your account be charged a fee for doing so? A final investigation is to review the bank's fee structure. How will its charges impact the mix of services that you expect from the bank? If you are investigating multiple banks, then look at these issues for the entire group, and then compare the outcome to determine which one will work best for you.

Another investing option provided by banks is the *certificate of deposit*. This is a term bank deposit with a fixed duration and a stated interest rate. In essence, it is a promissory note issued by a bank. This instrument normally pays a fixed interest rate upon maturity, though some variable-rate versions are available. A more restrictive CD may impose an early-withdrawal penalty (which can be quite large). Given the low interest rate offered for CDs and the restricted nature of early withdrawals, this is generally not a recommended lending arrangement for an investor. If you insist on parking money in a certificate of deposit, then at least shop around first – the differences in interest rates offered can be substantial.

Money Market Funds

A good alternative to a bank is the *money market fund*. These funds are a type of mutual fund that restricts its investments to highly liquid, near-term instruments. They mostly invest in debt securities with high credit ratings and short maturities, such as United States government debt issuances and short-term debt issued by large corporations. Their investment strategy is to offer investors a high level of liquidity, coupled with a very low risk level. In addition, the principal investment in a money market fund does not change in value.

> **Tip:** Most money market fund managers invest in approximately the same securities, so the returns generated by the funds will be about the same. Therefore, to improve your return on investment, select a fund that has a lower operating expense charge.

The convenience offered by money market funds is quite comparable to that of banks, while offering better returns on investment. For example (and depending on the fund), an investor can write checks on her money market fund. Better yet, some of these funds offer tax-free investments, which can be a considerable attraction for those investors in high tax brackets. Other funds offer a debit card, so that you can withdraw cash from the local ATM.

Tip: Use a money market fund to park cash that you plan to repurpose in the near future. For example, if you plan to use dollar cost averaging to slowly invest an inheritance in the stock market, then this is a good place to safely invest the money in the meantime. Or, if you want to maintain a cash reserve for emergencies, this is a good place to keep the money.

Tip: If you are in a high tax bracket, it can make sense to invest in a tax-free money market account. Otherwise, your already-low dividends will receive a tax haircut that results in negligible returns. This is less of an issue if you are investing from within a tax-shielded retirement account.

There is a downside to money market funds, which is that they are not insured by the federal government. However, this is not a major concern, since it is quite difficult for fund investments to decline. In the rare cases where a decline in fund value occurred, the amount of the decline was in the low single digits.

Bonds

A bond is a fixed obligation to pay that is issued by a corporation or government entity to investors. Bonds usually include a periodic interest payment, and are paid off as of a specific maturity date. The interest rates paid on bonds are higher than banks offer for saving accounts and certificates of deposit, and also exceed the rates on money market funds.

The main downside to investing in bonds is that the issuer could go bankrupt. If so, your invested funds may be lost. However, as long as you only invest in highly-rated bonds, the probability of issuer default is quite low. This issue can also be mitigated by investing in a bond fund rather than in individual bonds, so that your investment is spread across many bond issuers.

Another risk associated with bonds is that their resale value can decline as interest rates rise. This is because newer bonds must be offered at higher interest rates, which reduces the demand for your bonds that were issued at lower interest rates. The result is that, if you need to sell a bond before its maturity date, the amount you can obtain for it will be less than its face amount. However, this issue is not a concern if you intend to hold the bond until its maturity date, since it can then be redeemed for its full face amount.

Given the considerations just noted, you should only invest in bonds under certain circumstances. One possibility is when you want to earn a specific amount of income for an extended period of time, since issuers pay out specific amounts of cash at fixed intervals for interest payments. Another possibility is when you need to park the money for a fairly extended period of time, after which it will be spent. For example, if you need to replace production equipment in five years for $100,000, then invest the money in bonds now, in expectation of using the funds in five years. Yet another scenario is to diversify away from your stock investments; this is because bonds tend to appreciate in value when the stock market declines.

Types of Bonds

There are many types of bonds. The list below contains several of the more common types:

- *Convertible bond.* A convertible bond can be converted into the common stock of the issuer at a predetermined conversion ratio. This can yield a significant gain for the investor if the common stock price of the issuer increases substantially. However, these bonds pay a reduced interest rate, which investors are willing to accept on the grounds that the conversion feature has some value.
- *Deferred interest bond.* A deferred interest bond offers little or no interest at the start of the bond term, and more interest near the end. This format is useful for businesses that currently have little cash with which to pay interest.
- *Income bond.* With an income bond, the issuer is only obligated to make interest payments to bond holders if the issuer or a specific project earns a profit. If the bond terms allow for cumulative interest, then the unpaid interest will accumulate until such time as there is sufficient income to pay the amounts owed.
- *Serial bond.* A serial bond is gradually paid off in each successive year, so the total amount of debt outstanding is gradually reduced.
- *Variable rate bond.* The interest rate paid on a variable rate bond varies with a baseline indicator, which is usually a well-known interest rate.
- *Zero coupon bond.* No interest is paid on a zero coupon bond. Instead, investors buy this bond at a large discount to its face value in order to earn a return on it when it is eventually redeemed. The value of these bonds can drop rapidly if the Fed raises interest rates, so only people with a strong tolerance for risk should purchase them.

Bond Features

Additional features can be added to a bond to make it easier to sell to investors at a higher price. These features are noted below:

- *Sinking fund.* The issuer creates a sinking fund to which cash is periodically added, and which is used to ensure that bonds are eventually redeemed. This feature reduces default risk.
- *Conversion feature.* Bonds holders have the option to convert their bonds into the stock of the issuer at a predetermined conversion ratio. This feature increases the potential return for the investor.
- *Guarantees.* The repayment of a bond may be guaranteed by a third party. This feature reduces default risk.

The following additional bond features favor the issuer, and so may reduce the price at which investors are willing to purchase bonds:

- *Call feature*. The issuer has the right to buy back bonds earlier than the stated maturity date.
- *Subordination*. Bond holders are positioned after more senior debt holders to be paid back from issuer assets in the event of a default.

<u>Bond Investment Considerations</u>

There are several issues to consider when making a bond selection. First, if you want to ensure that the price of the bond will remain relatively steady, then buy bonds that mature within the next few years. Since the term to maturity is quite short, changes in the market interest rate will have only a minor impact on the price at which these bonds can be sold in the interim. Conversely, if you plan to hold a bond to maturity, then the number of years remaining is less of a consideration, since you will be obtaining its full face value when it is redeemed by the issuer. If you have no qualms about investing in bonds over the long term, then review the related yield curve (see next) to see if issuers are currently paying a higher interest rate on long-term bonds (which is usually the case). If not, it makes more sense to invest in shorter-term bonds with higher interest rates.

Another investing consideration is how likely a bond issuer is to default. This risk is reviewed by a credit rating agency, which assigns credit ratings to either the issuers of certain kinds of debt, or directly to their debt instruments. There are three major credit rating agencies that provide ratings for the bulk of all debt issuances. They are authorized for ratings work as Nationally Recognized Statistical Rating Organizations (NRSROs) by the SEC. The three agencies that collectively control most of the market are:

- Moody's Investor Service
- Standard & Poor's
- Fitch Ratings

The ratings issued by these agencies are used by investors to determine the price at which to buy bonds. It is difficult to issue bonds without a credit rating, since the issuance might otherwise be undersubscribed or can only be sold at a high interest rate.

The rating classifications used by the agencies vary from each other to some extent. The following table presents a comparison of the credit rating classifications of the three largest agencies. Bond issuances rated as investment grade in the table are considered suitable for investment purposes. The ratings classified as speculative are generally avoided by anyone looking for safe investments.

Credit Rating Comparison

Risk Level	Moody's	Standard & Poor's	Fitch
Investment grade:			
(highest investment grade)	Aaa	AAA	AAA
	Aa1	AA+	AA+
	Aa2	AA	AA
	Aa3	AA-	AA-
	A1	A+	A+
	A2	A	A
	A3	A-	A-
	Baa1	BBB+	BBB+
	Baa2	BBB	BBB
(lowest investment grade)	Baa3	BBB-	BBB-
Speculative grade:			
(highest speculative grade)	Ba1	BB+	BB+
	Ba2	BB	BB
	Ba3	BB-	BB-
	B1	B+	B+
	B2	B	B
	B3	B-	B-
	Caa1	CCC+	CCC+

Note: There are additional lower speculative grades than those listed in this table.

Only a large company with a stable business model and conservative financial practices can hope to qualify for one of the top-tier investment grades. Indeed, so few AAA ratings are issued that the recipients tend to use them as marketing tools to impress customers, suppliers, and employees. Since the AAA rating is well out of reach for most companies, the primary goal is simply to obtain a mid-level investment grade rating. By doing so, investors will not demand an excessively high interest rate on bond issuances. Companies certainly do not want their bonds to be classified as speculative, since investors will not buy them unless the company is willing to pay a very high interest rate.

An issuer may find that the credit rating agencies assign different credit ratings to different bond issuances, even though the bonds are all being issued by the same entity. This variation is caused by differences in the amount of collateral (if any) assigned to the debt, the level of subordination to other debt instruments of the issuer, and other debt terms.

The Yield Curve

A *yield curve* is a graphical representation of the yields on a bond, based on its maturity date. A normal yield curve shows a gradual increase in yield for bonds that mature further in the future, since it is riskier to hold the bonds for a longer period of time. An inverted yield curve presents a declining yield for bonds with longer maturities, which is typically triggered by an expectation that a recession will occur in the future. A flat yield curve is most likely during economic transition periods, when investors are uncertain about whether rates will rise or fall.

Economists typically review the difference between the interest rate on the 10-year Treasury note and the federal funds rate, which is known as the interest rate spread. For example, if the federal funds rate is 1.50 percent and the 10-year Treasury note rate is yielding 3.25 percent, then the interest rate spread is 1.75 percent, or 175 basis points. This spread embodies the expectations of fixed-income traders about the economy, since their trading activity is setting the yield on the 10-year Treasury note.

When there is a steep yield curve (a large interest rate spread), this is a significant indicator of economic weakness. It typically arises when the Federal Reserve tries to counter a period of economic weakness by lowering its overnight rate, which lowers borrowing costs and therefore encourages lending, which in turn is presumably used to make purchases and fire up the economy. The problem is that the low overnight rate triggers inflationary concerns among fixed-income traders, since inflation lowers the value of principal and interest payments to be received in the future from bonds. Given this concern, the traders sell off their longer-term bond holdings, which are at most risk of a reduction in value from inflation, which lowers their prices and raises their yields. The net effect of these actions is that there is a greater interest rate spread, with a lower short-term rate and a higher yield on longer-term instruments – which represents a steeper yield curve.

The reverse situation can also arise. The Fed may choose to raise interest rates in order to cool off a hot economy, since the higher rate restricts borrowing and therefore dampens purchases. This reduces the risk of long-term inflation, so fixed-income traders are more likely to buy longer-term bonds, thereby raising their prices and lowering their yields. The end result is a flatter yield curve, since the short-term interest rate is rising, while the long-term rate is falling. When this reversal is accelerated, the yield curve can become inverted, where short-term rates are higher than long-term rates. An inverted yield curve is a reasonable predictor of a recession, since the fixed-income traders are expecting a weak economy in the future, which encourages their expectations of low interest rates over the longer-term. The inverted yield curve is not a perfect predictor of a recession, since it has predicted several recessions that did not occur.

U.S. Government Debt Instruments

Despite the continuing increases in the debt of the United States government, its debt instruments are still considered among the lowest-risk in the world. The ones most commonly used by corporations for investment are Treasury Bills (T-Bills) and Treasury Notes (T-Notes). T-Bills have 3, 6, and 12-month maturities. T-Bills having maturities of 3 and 6 months and are auctioned on a weekly basis, while T-Bills with 12-month maturities are auctioned once a month. T-Bills are sold at a discount, and redeemed upon maturity at their face value. There is a very active secondary market in T-Bills, so it is easy to sell them prior to their maturity dates.

The maturities of T-Notes range from 1 to 10 years. Two-year T-Notes are issued on a monthly basis, while T-Notes with other maturities are issued on a quarterly basis. T-Notes are available as both inflation-indexed and fixed-rate investments. Interest on T-Notes is paid semi-annually. T-Notes are traded on secondary markets at premiums or discounts to their face values, to reflect the current market interest rate.

Treasury Bonds are also available. Bonds have similar characteristics to T-Notes, but have longer maturities. Maturities are generally in the range of 10 to 30 years.

The government also offers Treasury Inflation-Protected Security (TIPS), which is a Treasury bond that is indexed to an inflationary gauge; doing so protects investors from the decline in the purchasing power of their money. The principal value of TIPS rises as inflation increases, while the interest payment varies with the adjusted principal value of the bond. However, because of the value of this inflation protection feature, the TIPS interest rate is relatively low.

Paradoxically, the trouble with U.S. government debt instruments is their safety – the United States government can obtain the lowest possible interest rates, so there is little return on funds invested in these instruments.

State and Local Government Debt

An interesting investment option is the debt obligations issued by state and local governments. These debt instruments are usually issued in conjunction with the revenue streams associated with large capital projects, such as airport fees and tolls from toll roads. Other instruments are based on general tax revenues. The maturities of these obligations are typically multi-year, so an investor in need of cash must rely upon a vigorous aftermarket to liquidate them prior to their maturity dates. The returns on state and local debt obligations are higher than the yields on federal government issuances, and income from these investments is usually exempt from federal and state taxation. This exemption feature means that these obligations are of great interest to those investors in high tax brackets.

Though it is rare for a state or local government to default on its debt, such cases are not unknown, so be mindful of the reliability of the cash flows supporting debt repayment.

Corporate Bonds

Many larger corporations issue bonds. The interest paid on these bonds is taxable, so a good way to invest in them is from within a retirement account. By doing so, the taxes on any interest income will be deferred. Alternatively, investors in lower tax brackets may invest in corporate bonds without the protection of a retirement account, since the resulting taxes will be relatively low.

How to Buy Bonds

Bonds can be purchased either individually or through a bond fund that contains a selection of bonds. It is generally better to invest in a bond fund, for several reasons. First, the managers of a bond fund will diversify its holdings for you, which is more difficult to do when you are purchasing individual bonds. This diversification covers not just types of bonds, but also their maturities – a bond fund will invest in bonds with a range of maturity dates. Second, the cost to acquire individual bonds is high, sometimes reaching two percent on small purchases. This cost can be hidden, where some brokers include the commission in the price of the bond. Alternatively, the fee charged by a bond fund is usually in the vicinity of ½% per year, which is much more cost-effective. And finally, deciding which bonds to purchase requires a lot of research time to determine the financial viability of the issuer; it is easier to shift this task onto fund managers.

When researching which bonds to buy, a standard set of information will be provided. Explanations for several of these items are noted in the following table, alongside the actual information posted for a bond issued by Xcel Energy, which is a regional electricity provider.

Explanations of Bond Terms

	Terms	Explanation
Issuer	Xcel Energy, Inc.	The name of the bond issuer
Ratings	BB+/Baa1/BBB+	These are the credit ratings issued for the bonds by the various credit rating agencies
Amount	$500 million	The total amount of the bond issuance
Coupon	1.75%	The interest rate that the issuer will pay on the bonds; it is a percent of the maturity value of the bonds
Price	99.777	The current market price of the bonds; it is calculated as the coupon rate divided by the current price
Yield	1.794%	The effective interest rate earned; this is higher than the coupon rate, since the purchase price of the bonds is lower than the face amount
Spread	T+62	The difference between the yield on this bond and the yield on a Treasury bond, expressed as the number of basis points difference
Maturity	March 15, 2027	The date on which the bonds mature

If you want to keep the risk level to a minimum, a good choice is United States Treasury bonds, which are considered to have essentially no risk of default. Of course, the downside of acquiring an investment with no risk is that the return on investment is quite low. Nonetheless, there is a huge market for these bonds. While it is possible to purchase Treasury bonds directly from the United States Treasury (through its treasurydirect.gov website), there are advantages to buying these bonds through your brokerage account. By doing so, you can more easily see the full range of your investments in one place. Also, it is easier to sell Treasury bonds through the broker.

If you choose not to invest through a bond fund or to buy Treasury bonds, then the risk of making a purchase that you will regret increases dramatically. However, there are several best practices to consider that can reduce this risk. Consider the following:

- *Avoid salespeople*. When a brokerage salesperson calls you with a bond buying recommendation, hang up at once. These people are typically on 100% commission compensation plans, so they will push anything in order to make a living. It is much better to do your own research and then buy bonds through a broker that does not employ these salespeople.
- *Buy quality*. Always buy bonds from issuers in excellent financial condition. These issuers also pay rock-bottom interest rates on their bonds, but at least they (almost) never go bankrupt. You can certainly take a chance on a high-yield bond issued by firms in difficult financial condition – but don't be surprised when they default.
- *Diversify holdings*. Economic conditions may impact one industry harder than another, so invest in a range of bonds from issuers located in different industries. Generally, try to cap your bond investment at no more than 5% of the total amount invested in one bond. This means that you should be invested in at least 20 bonds from different issuers. Given this level of diversification, it is easier to just invest in a bond fund.
- *Look for a call feature*. If a bond has a call feature, the issuer can redeem it prior to its maturity date. This is a concern when the interest rate on the bond is a good one, since you may only be able to enjoy the related coupon payments for a short period of time. Generally, try to invest in bonds that have no call feature, or for which the call feature is not activated until a number of years have passed.

Summary

The main problem with lending arrangements is that the interest rate paid is relatively low, especially in comparison to the returns you can receive from stock investments. To enhance the return on these arrangements, use bond funds that have low operating expenses. Their managers will diversify their bond holdings for you, and the low expenses will not cut too deeply into your returns. In addition, try to invest in bonds from within a retirement account, so that the taxes on any income are deferred. These steps can maximize your returns while keeping the associated default risk down to a manageable level.

Chapter 6
Investing in Funds

Introduction

Enormous sums have been invested in both mutual funds and exchange-traded funds, and for good reason. They are an efficient way to invest, are relatively inexpensive, and represent an easy way to diversify your holdings. In this chapter, we compare these fund types, discuss best practices for fund investing, and delve into several related topics.

Mutual Funds vs. Exchange-Traded Funds

The two main types of funds are mutual funds and exchange-traded funds (ETFs). It can be useful to understand what they are, and the differences between them.

A mutual fund is a type of financial vehicle that allows you to pool your money with funds provided by other investors to purchase a collection of stocks, bonds, or other securities. Mutual funds tend to concentrate in either stocks, bonds, or the money market. This collection of investments is known as a portfolio. The price of a mutual fund, which is also known as its net asset value, is calculated as the total value of the securities in the portfolio, divided by the number of the fund's outstanding shares. This price varies constantly, as both the values of the securities and the number of shares outstanding changes.

> **Note:** Mutual fund investors do not actually own the securities in which a fund invests; they only own shares in the fund itself.

If a mutual fund is actively managed, buy and sell decisions are made by its managers and researchers. Their performance benchmark is usually to outperform a well-known index, such as the Standard & Poor's 500 – ideally over a multi-year timeline.

When selecting a mutual fund, the quality of its managers is a consideration. They should come from the top business schools, be certified as Chartered Financial Analysts, and have years of experience in the industry. A high-quality team has deep experience in selected industries, pores over financial statements, meets with company managers to discuss their strategies, and generally has a better understanding of where stocks are undervalued or overvalued.

An essential advantage of using a mutual fund is its level of diversification. The typical fund invests in anywhere from several dozen to over a hundred securities, all spread across different sectors. This level of diversification allows them the opportunity to achieve excellent returns at relatively low risk.

Another advantage of using a mutual fund is the ease with which trades can be conducted. It is usually possible to invest in a fund online, and to issue a withdrawal notification in the same way. Also, if the fund is a money market fund, it may provide check-writing privileges, which means that your access to invested funds is quite similar to what you would have through the local bank – though usually while earning a somewhat higher return on your invested funds.

An exchange-traded fund is a basket of securities that can be bought or sold through a brokerage. ETFs have been constructed for every conceivable asset class, including bonds, gold, and high technology stocks. ETFs are also offered that can enhance your investment leverage, engage in short markets, and avoid short-term capital gains taxes.

An ETF is bought and sold in the same manner as company stock, which means that it has a ticker symbol and price data that can be viewed throughout the trading day. However, unlike company stock, the number of ETF shares outstanding will change every day, due to the continual creation of new shares and redemption of existing ones.

Examples of the types of ETFs currently available are as follows:

- *Bond ETFs.* These funds invest in all types of bonds, including corporate bonds, international bonds, municipal bonds, and U.S. Treasury bonds.
- *Commodity ETFs.* These funds track the price of a commodity, such as gold or corn.
- *Foreign market ETFs.* These funds track markets outside of the United States.
- *Industry ETFs.* These funds invest in specific industries, such as high technology or pharmaceuticals.
- *Market ETFs.* These funds track a specific index, such as the Standard & Poor's 500.
- *Style ETFs.* These funds track an investment style or have a market capitalization focus, such as only investing in small-cap growth stocks.

In addition, a few ETFs are actively managed, which means that they are intended to outperform an index, rather than merely tracking its results.

There are multiple advantages to ETFs. First, they are easy to trade. They can be bought and sold throughout the trading day, while mutual funds only trade at the end of the day. Also, the holdings of an ETF are very transparent, since they are required to publish their holdings every day. Further, ETFs tend to generate fewer capital gain distributions than actively-managed mutual funds. Yet another advantage is their low cost. The operating costs of both ETFs and mutual funds are relatively low and are spread across thousands of investors, so their fees are low. In particular, the trading costs of these funds are much lower than any individual investor can obtain. Finally, since ETFs are traded like stocks, investors can place limit orders (as discussed in the next chapter) that are not available for mutual funds.

There are also some disadvantages to ETFs. First, if an ETF is not frequently traded, there can be a wide bid-ask spread, where investors buy at the high price of the spread and sell at the low price of the spread. Also, ETF sales are not settled for two business days following the sale transaction, which means that the resulting funds are not available for reinvestment for two days.

Both mutual funds and ETFs are extremely safe investments. This is because they maintain a dollar's worth of securities for every dollar invested. Therefore, if you want to withdraw your money from one of these funds, you will receive the current market value of that investment. If the market value of the securities acquired by the fund has declined, then you may receive somewhat less than you invested – but you will not lose your entire investment.

Fund Investment Best Practices

While funds are generally a good vehicle for investing your money, there are various best practices available that will increase your odds of generating a greater return on investment, as well as of avoiding losses. These best practices are noted in the following sub-sections.

Reduce Fund Costs

Your rate of return will be deeply impacted by the operating expenses charged by a fund. Even small differences in these charges can build up to major differences in investment returns over time. Therefore, comparison shop among funds to see which ones have a combination of good management and low fees. Typically, a bond fund should charge less than ½% per year, while a stock fund should charge less than 1%. There are several costs to monitor, as noted in the following bullet points:

- It is essential to minimize the *sales load*, which is the commission charged to an investor when buying shares in a mutual fund. If a sales load is charged, then look for alternative funds in which to invest. No-load funds do not have a commission expense associated with them. It is useful to remember that this commission goes to the broker selling you on the fund, not the fund managers. Therefore, it is irrational to assume that a load fund will generate a better return on investment than a no-load fund. In fact, given the added expense of a load fund, its subsequent return on investment will probably be lower than you would have experienced with a no-load fund. In addition, given the presence of a commission, the broker has a strong incentive to push you to invest in a load fund, even when your financial situation clearly indicates that an alternative strategy is warranted.
- Avoid a *back-end load*, which is a fee paid when selling mutual fund shares. It can be a flat fee or gradually decrease over time, usually within five to 10 years. The fund managers make money by using the gradual reduction in the back-end load to convince investors to stay in the fund for a long time, while they charge high annual fees. Once again, this is a commission, which is an unnecessary expense.
- *Minimize operating expenses.* All funds accumulate operating expenses, which are charged through to investors as a deduction from the share price. Over the long term, differences in the expenses charged can have a very noticeable impact on your return on investment. Therefore, it makes sense to favor funds with lower operating expenses.

- *Try index funds.* Index funds require minimal management, since they merely invest in an index (such as the S&P 500), seeking to match the performance of that index. No expenses are incurred to engage in research activities. This means that its operating expenses should be extremely low, which benefits the investor.

Note: Index funds are capitalization weighted, which means that the stocks in the fund are held in proportion to their market values within the associated index. If some stocks within an index have inflated valuations, then the associated index fund is forced to invest in a higher proportion of those stocks. If you are uncomfortable with this situation, then invest in an index fund that gives equal weight to all the stocks in the associated index.

Look for Consistent Returns

Some fund managers can generate extraordinary returns for a short period of time, usually by allocating funds toward riskier investments. However, they are more likely to generate significant losses over the longer term, as these investments occasionally perform quite poorly. The result is a high degree of variability in their returns, especially when the market as a whole declines. A better approach is to look for consistent returns within a less risky portfolio of investments. There will still be historical variability in the returns, but not to such an excessive degree.

Avoid Taxes

Invest in funds that do not buy and sell securities very frequently, such as index funds. These funds hold onto investments for long periods of time, resulting in few short-term gains that would be taxed at a higher rate than long-term capital gains.

Allocate Assets

A prudent strategy is to decide upon – and hold to – the percentage of your funds that will be placed in an investment category. For example, you might invest 30% in bond funds, 50% in mutual funds, and 20% in real estate. This allocation is mostly based on your age. When you are younger and so have lots of years in which to weather the vagaries of the stock market, it makes sense to allocate a larger proportion of your assets to the stock market. As retirement approaches, you will probably want to experience more certainty in your returns, so a higher percentage of assets is shifted into bonds. Within each of these allocations, further diversify into different investments. For example, a 50% investment in stocks might then be divvied up into funds that specialize in large-cap stocks, international stocks, and a stock index. By spreading your money among several funds that employ different investing strategies, you can gain from the expertise of fund managers that specialize in different aspects of the market.

Avoid Leveraged Funds

A leveraged fund uses financial derivatives and debt to amplify the return of an underlying index. This strategy can cause problems, because it can lead to significant gains, but also equally large losses. Given the volatility of these funds, they should be avoided.

Invest in Experience

Fund managers with significant experience in the field tend to perform better than those that do not. This is not an overriding factor in selecting a fund, but it can make sense to compare the experience levels of the teams assigned to the management of various funds.

Stock Fund Fundamentals

When investing in stock funds, there are several issues to be aware of. First, only select a fund that invests in a sufficiently large number of stocks. If a fund manager is only invested in 10 stocks, then a catastrophic decline in just one of them will have a major negative impact on the fund's returns. Conversely, if the manager had spread invested funds among 100 stocks, then a few major declines will have little impact.

Another issue to be aware of is how you make money through a stock fund. One way is through the dividends received from the issuers of the stocks held by the fund. The fund manager passes these dividends through to you, or gives you the option to reinvest them in the fund. Unless you need the money, it is better to keep reinvesting the funds, thereby growing your investment stake in the fund. Another way to make money is from capital gain distributions from the fund, which occur when the fund sells stocks for more than their purchase price. As was the case with dividends, you can opt to reinvest these gains in the fund. And finally, the price per share of the fund can increase if the value of its stock holdings increases. This price per share is only a paper profit until such time as you choose to sell the shares. When aggregated, these three sources comprise your total return on investment.

Fund managers invest in accordance with the operating guidelines of the fund, which state its criteria for investment. For example, the guidelines for one fund might state that it only invests in overseas large-cap stocks, while the guidelines for another fund mandate that it invest in small-cap growth stocks. When selecting funds, be sure to peruse their posted summaries of investment guidelines, to better understand what you will be investing in.

Note: Large-cap stocks refer to companies with market capitalizations exceeding $10 billion. Medium-cap stocks refer to companies with market capitalizations between $2 billion and $10 billion, while small-cap stocks refer to companies with market capitalizations between $300 million and $2 billion. Micro-cap stocks refer to companies with market capitalizations below $300 million.

There are different types of investment strategies that a stock fund manager can pursue. For example, an income fund primarily targets stocks that pay out high dividends, while growth funds invest in smaller-cap businesses that are growing rapidly (and which may not be paying dividends at all). Other funds, known as growth and income funds, strike a balance between these extremes, seeking to maximize both stock price growth and dividends. It makes sense to invest in several funds that are targeted at different investment strategies. This might mean that you are investing in both a small-cap growth fund and a large-cap income fund. By doing so, you are spreading your bets across several fund managers and investment strategies.

When investing in international funds, an area of concern is whether a fund is investing in an excessively narrowly-defined region. It is generally not a good idea to invest in a fund that is concentrated within one country, because an economic downturn within a smaller country can have a heavy impact on all stocks associated with that area. A better choice is to invest in an international fund that is broader in scope, perhaps one that invests everywhere outside the United States, or which focuses on a specific region, such as all of South America or Africa. A further issue to be aware of with international stock funds is the impact of changes in the value of various currencies in relation to the U.S. dollar. Generally, a declining dollar valuation increases the value of international stock funds, while a rising dollar decreases their value. International funds can hedge against these valuation changes, but hedges cost money, which increases the operating costs of the fund.

Bond Fund Fundamentals

When investing in bond funds, there are several issues to be aware of. As was the case with stock funds, only select a fund that invests in a sufficiently large number of bonds. Otherwise, a default by one issuer can have an inordinate impact on the returns from a bond fund.

The prices of bond funds tend to be relatively stable when they only invest in short-term bonds. Funds that invest in longer-term bonds are more subject to fluctuations in interest rates. This means that short-term bond funds are a good investment when you want to park some money for a short period of time without having to worry about it declining in value in the interim. In addition, these funds generate a somewhat higher rate of return than money market funds. For example, if you are building up a cash reserve to be used as the down payment on a house a few years from now, a good place to park the money is in a short-term bond fund.

A key aspect of the prices of bond funds is that they move in opposition to interest rates. For example, if interest rates fall, this increases the prices of pre-existing bonds, since they were issued with higher interest rates than the current market rate. Conversely, when interest rates increase, the prices of pre-existing bonds fall, because they now return a lower rate than the current market rate. This means that the prices of bond funds rise and fall in accordance with where market interest rates are at the moment. This also means that you should not buy into a bond fund just because it has a recent history of good performance – that may have more to do with interest rates than the performance of the fund's manager.

> **Tip:** A good way to review the performance of a bond fund is to compare its results to the performance of similar funds with the same investment guidelines. When conducting this comparison, use the *SEC yield* calculation, which approximates the yield an investor would receive in a year by assuming that bonds in the portfolio are held to maturity, all income reinvested, and all fees and expenses factored in.

When comparing the yields advertised by bond funds, be aware that funds play tricks with the yield formulation to make their results look better than those of the competition. First, they may waive some or all of their operating expense charges for a period of time, which amps up their reported yield. This is an especially common trick among new funds that are trying to gain traction in the marketplace. Another trick is to invest a portion of its cash in riskier bonds that have a slightly higher rate of return. These investments may be borderline outside of the stated investment guidelines of the fund. A third trick is to increase the maturities of the bonds in which it invests, which results in a slightly higher interest rate. When a fund engages in several of these practices at once, it can appear to produce significantly better results than competing funds, allowing it to attract more investor funds.

An especially good reason to avoid load funds is that, given the extra fees charged, their managers are under extra pressure to provide good performance to investors. This pressure can lead them to invest aggressively, such as by investing in lower-quality bonds in the expectation that the economy will improve, which will raise the value of these bonds. If these fund managers are incorrect in their assumptions, then their funds are at increased risk of producing poor results. In short, more costly funds can actually return worse results than lower-cost funds whose managers simply buy and hold bonds for the long term.

Bond Fund Selection Process

There are several steps to go through when deciding upon the right bond fund for you. The first step is to keep your costs down, thereby enhancing your long-term returns. This means selecting a fund that has low operating costs – of which there are not many. Fee structures tend to be high, so eliminating high-cost funds from consideration will likely eliminate 90% of the available funds.

The second step in the selection process is to determine the length to maturity that you want, and then review the investment guidelines of the remaining funds to determine which ones meet your criteria. For example, a short-term bond fund invests in bonds with maturities of less than five years, while an intermediate-term fund invests in bonds with maturity dates that are between two and 10 years, and a long-term fund invests in bonds with maturity dates of ten years or more. The yields generated from a short-term bond fund are the lowest, while those from a long-term fund are the highest. Investing in intermediate-term and long-term funds makes the most sense when you intend to invest your funds for a long period of time, and are willing to tolerate more volatility in the value of the bond fund. The values of long-term bond funds are the most volatile, so only invest here if you are comfortable with a higher degree of uncertainty.

Once you have found a set of lower-cost bond funds that invest in bonds with the right maturities, review the credit ratings of the bonds in which they invest. Bonds with a poor credit rating generate a higher return, while bonds with excellent credit ratings generate a lower return. The choice is up to you, based on how much risk you are willing to tolerate.

Finally, review the taxability of the interest being passed through to you. Taxable interest is fine, as long as you are investing funds from a tax-deferred retirement account. If that is not the case, and especially if you are in a high tax bracket, then tax-free bonds might be a better choice.

In short, there are a number of selection criteria to work through before you can select a bond fund that works best for your specific needs.

Hybrid Funds

A variation on stock funds and bond funds is a fund that invests in both areas, which is called a hybrid fund. These funds are not limited to just stocks and bonds. For example, a hybrid fund might invest in stocks and real estate, or bonds and gold.

A hybrid fund is targeted at achieving greater diversification, thereby reducing investment risk. The level of risk associated with a fund is based on its investing guidelines, which may vary from conservative to aggressive.

There are several variations on the concept. A balanced fund follows a standard asset allocation proportion, such as 60% in stocks and 40% in bonds. A blended fund includes a mix of value and growth stocks. A target date fund begins with a more aggressive allocation, and then gradually rebalances to a more conservative allocation, to be used by a specific date in the future. In the last case, the asset allocation proportion will change over time. In all cases, the fund manager actively manages the individual asset holdings within each asset category to respond to changes in market conditions, as well as to take advantage of possible capital appreciation opportunities.

Summary

We advocate the use of funds, and especially the use of multiple funds, because they allow you to diversify your money among a large number of investments. By doing so, a few failures will be offset by gains elsewhere in your portfolio. A further advantage of funds is that they are professionally managed and (depending on the fund) are relatively inexpensive. This means that you can benefit from expert advice without spending too much for the privilege. In short, investing in funds is an excellent choice.

Chapter 7
Working with Brokerage Firms

Introduction

It is much easier to engage in investing activities when you are working through a brokerage firm. These entities can conduct buy and sell orders on your behalf, and have online tracking systems that make it much easier to centralize your investment record keeping and performance tracking. In this chapter, we describe the types of brokerage firms, why you should use one, and several related topics.

Types of Brokerage Firms

A *stockbroker* is a financial professional who executes buy and sell orders in the market on behalf of clients. The typical stockbroker works for a brokerage firm and processes transactions for a number of clients. This person is typically paid on a commission basis, though it may be mixed with a modest base salary. From the investor's perspective, dealing with stockbrokers who are compensated on a commission basis can be a problem, since these people have a monetary incentive to convince you to constantly churn your investment portfolio.

There are two main types of brokerage firms. One is the *discount broker*, which carries out buy and sell orders for a low commission rate. In order to keep costs low, these brokers offer their services either mostly or entirely over the Internet, thereby eliminating the cost of retail branches (though the larger ones still maintain some offices). In order to charge this low rate (or none at all), a discount broker cannot afford to have any research staff or investment advisors, which means that most clients never speak to anyone at the brokerage firm at all. If you need to talk to someone, it can be difficult to reach customer support staff within a short period of time. Nonetheless, it is now quite common for investors to obtain investment advice from a third party and then conduct their own buy and sell transactions through a discount broker.

> **Tip:** An advantage of working with a discount brokerage is that you are unlikely to deal with anyone who is on a commission basis, and therefore wants to convince you to make purchases that may not be in your best interests. Instead, these businesses are primarily order execution platforms.

> **Tip:** Before signing up with a discount broker that charges no commissions at all, be aware that they have to make money somehow. They do this by charging for ancillary services, such as charging to move your account balance to another broker, as well as for upgraded services, wire transfers, and paper statements. They may also earn interest on the uninvested portion of your funds. Consequently, always evaluate the entire package of services before opting for free trading.

The other brokerage type is the *full-service broker*, which provides the full range of services to its clients, such as retirement and tax planning, as well as analysis reports on various securities. In exchange for these services, a full-service broker charges a much higher commission for securities trades than discount brokers.

If you have minimal investing knowledge and/or complicated financial goals, it can make more sense to use a full-service brokerage. Or, if you prefer to deal with someone in person, then pick a brokerage that has an office near you. Another reason to use a full-service brokerage is if you have a history of making poor (and perhaps impulsive) investment decisions. If so, it makes sense to use an investment advisor as a filter, to block out your worst impulses before executing a trade. Alternatively, if your financial situation is relatively simple and you have firm investment goals, then a discount brokerage may be a reasonable choice for you.

Both discounters and full-service firms offer their own mutual funds, as well as access to outside funds. A fee is usually charged if you want to access outside funds, whereas buy and sell transactions involving their in-house funds are generally free.

Advantages of Using a Brokerage Firm

There are some specific advantages associated with using a brokerage firm. First, though it is possible to buy some assets directly, it makes sense to buy through a brokerage, so that you can track all of your investments from one dashboard. By centralizing your investments, you can also track the original purchase price, current market values, and rate of return on each investment. You can also place all buy and sell orders through your brokerage, which means that you only have to become accustomed to one system interface, rather than several. And, if you are working with a full-service brokerage, then you may end up dealing with an investment advisor for years who understands both your financial situation and how you want to invest. Furthermore, a brokerage will allow you to easily shift excess funds into a money market account until they are needed. In short, there are several excellent reasons that drive any investor to work with a brokerage firm.

Market Orders and Limit Orders

When placing an order with a broker, there are two types of orders that you can specify. One is the *market order*, which is an order to buy or sell a stock at the best available price. Generally, this type of order will be executed at once. However, the price at which the order will be executed is not guaranteed. This approach is the most common, but can be a bit risky when there is little trading volume in a stock; in this situation, the price at which the trade is settled may not be to your liking.

The alternative is the *limit order*, where the transaction is only to be completed at a specific price or better. For a buy limit order, the order will be executed only at the limit price or a lower one, while for sell limit orders, it will be executed only at the limit price or higher.

Securities Investors Protection Corporation

When dealing with brokerages, it may be comforting to know that a portion of your funds parked at these entities is protected. The Securities Investors Protection Corporation (SIPC) provides insurance coverage to the clients of brokerage firms. The SIPC also oversees the liquidation of brokerage firms that go bankrupt or are in financial difficulties. The SIPC's main goal is to return funds to investors as soon as possible. However, it does not provide complete protection; instead, it covers $500,000 of the cash and securities held by a brokerage for each investor, of which the cap on cash balances is $250,000. Some brokerages purchase additional insurance, so that substantially more investor funds are covered.

Summary

In-depth investing activity requires the services of a brokerage firm. Your main choices are to go with a discount brokerage or a full-service one. However, these are merely descriptions of two general types of brokerage firms, when in reality there is a broader range of brokerage firms, providing anywhere from the bare minimum of services to very high-end concierge-grade investment support. Consequently, it makes sense to review the offerings of a range of brokerages, to determine which one offers the exact mix of services and pricing that works best for you.

Chapter 8
The Interpretation of Financial Statements

Introduction

An investor who wants to learn about a business usually begins by inspecting its financial statements. The financial statements include three documents, which are the balance sheet, income statement, and statement of cash flows, as well as a set of accompanying footnotes. These documents describe the financial results, financial position, and cash flows of an organization. In the following pages, we discuss how to interpret the information contained within these statements, so that you can make better investment decisions.

Interpreting the Balance Sheet

A *balance sheet* (also known as a statement of financial position) presents information about an entity's assets, liabilities, and shareholders' equity, where the compiled result must match this formula, which is called the accounting equation:

$$\text{Total assets} = \text{Total liabilities} + \text{Equity}$$

This equation drives the name of the document, where the total of all assets must balance the total amount of liabilities and equity. This balancing concept is necessary, since the ownership of an asset can only occur if an organization either pays for it with an obligation (such as a loan) or with the funds invested by shareholders or the ongoing profits of the business (which is equity).

In essence, a balance sheet describes what a business owns, what it owes, and what residual amount net of the first two items is left over for its shareholders. It is used to assess an entity's liquidity and ability to pay its debts.

The balance sheet reports the aggregate effect of transactions as of a specific date. For example, if a balance sheet has been produced as part of a package of financial statements for the month of April, the information contained within the balance sheet is as of April 30, which is the last day of the month. Thus, it essentially represents a snapshot of the financial condition of a business as of a moment in time.

The basic format of a balance sheet is noted in the following exhibit. It contains a header, which describes the name of the entity whose financial information is being reported on, the name of the report, and the date as of which the report was constructed. In the following line items, we have noted how each one adds up into the various subtotals and totals in the document.

Sample Balance Sheet Format

Lowry Locomotion
Balance Sheet
As of December 31, 20X1

ASSETS	
Current assets	
Cash	A
Investments	B
Accounts receivable	C
Inventory	D
Prepaid expenses	E
Total current assets	A + B + C + D + E = F
Non-current assets	
Fixed assets	G
Goodwill	H
Other assets	I
Total non-current assets	G + H + I = J
Total assets	F + J
LIABILITIES AND EQUITY	
Current liabilities	
Accounts payable	K
Other payables	L
Accrued liabilities	M
Unearned revenues	N
Total current liabilities	K + L + M + N = O
Noncurrent liabilities	
Long-term debt	P
Bonds payable	Q
Total noncurrent liabilities	P + Q = R
Total liabilities	O + R = S
Shareholders' equity	
Common stock	T
Preferred stock	U
Additional paid-in capital	V
Retained earnings	W
Treasury stock	X
Total shareholders' equity	T + U + V + W + X = Y
Total liabilities and shareholders' equity	S + Y

To see how these calculations are used in a balance sheet, the following example replaces the line item computations with numbers taken from the general ledger of a business.

Sample Balance Sheet with Numeric Presentation

Lowry Locomotion
Balance Sheet
As of December 31, 20X1

ASSETS	
Current assets	
Cash	$45,000
Investments	80,000
Accounts receivable	425,000
Inventory	415,000
Prepaid expenses	15,000
Total current assets	$980,000
Non-current assets	
Fixed assets	800,000
Goodwill	200,000
Other assets	20,000
Total non-current assets	$1,020,000
Total assets	$2,000,000
LIABILITIES AND EQUITY	
Current liabilities	
Accounts payable	$215,000
Other payables	30,000
Accrued liabilities	28,000
Unearned revenues	12,000
Total current liabilities	$285,000
Noncurrent liabilities	
Long-term debt	200,000
Bonds payable	350,000
Total noncurrent liabilities	550,000
Total liabilities	$835,000

Shareholders' equity	
Common stock	10,000
Preferred stock	50,000
Additional paid-in capital	320,000
Retained earnings	825,000
Treasury stock	-40,000
Total shareholders' equity	**$1,165,000**
Total liabilities and shareholders' equity	**$2,000,000**

Relevance of a Low Cash Figure

The cash line item in a balance sheet might contain an extremely low number, perhaps one that is even negative or exactly zero. What is the significance of these low cash figures, and can they be of concern? The following bullet points clarify what a low cash figure could imply:

- *Low cash coupled with a line of credit.* If the liabilities section of the balance sheet contains a line item for a line of credit, it is quite possible that a business is simply drawing down cash from its line of credit in order to pay its bills. Once its cash reserves are depleted, it accesses the line of credit for more cash and pays its bills again. This arrangement may not be an issue if a company has a highly seasonal business, where it uses up cash during part of the year and pays off its debt when sales peak. The best way to learn if this is the case is to obtain monthly financial statements and track the amount of line of credit usage by month, as well as sales levels.
- *Zero cash.* When the cash balance is exactly zero, this probably means that a business cut checks in advance of having the cash to do so. Thus, it has no money with which to pay its bills. At year end, the auditors force the company to create a journal entry that reverses a sufficient amount of these payables to bring the cash balance up to zero.
- *Negative cash.* As just noted, a negative cash balance means that an entity has paid out more check payments than it can cover with its available cash. While the auditors will force a business to alter its books to show a cash balance of zero, this may not happen during the preparation of the intervening monthly financial statements, resulting in negative balances.

In short, the danger posed by a low cash balance depends on the situation. It could simply be part of the normal operations for a seasonal business, or it could indicate that an organization is teetering on the edge of bankruptcy.

The Impact of Sales Growth on Cash

When reviewing the cash balance, a key consideration is the rate of growth of the business. When a business is growing rapidly, its ability to generate cash from operations will probably not be sufficient to fund the expenditures needed to invest in fixed assets, extend credit to new customers, or pay for increased amounts of inventory. For example, when a retail chain expands to a new location, it must pay for the new store and all of the inventory that is needed in the new location. If management is attempting to expand at a high rate of speed, then all of the on-hand cash will undoubtedly be used up in short order, requiring that external financing be obtained to continue the growth. In this situation, you should estimate the rate at which cash is being used and judge the extent to which management can continue to procure cash in order to re-plenish the bank account at regular intervals.

Conversely, if management is engaged in an orderly shutdown of certain aspects of a business, you may find that the company will soon be awash in cash. This condition can arise when facilities are sold off, receivables are collected, and inventory is liquidated.

Tip: The margins that a business earns on its sales are a significant driver of its ability to grow. For example, a software company experiences extremely high profit levels, and so generates so much cash that it can afford to grow rapidly without requiring any additional cash infusions. Conversely, an oil refiner must make massive capital investments to open a new facility, and so cannot grow as quickly.

Inherent Profit Margin

Before delving into the accounts receivable area, it is useful to understand how important this area may be to a business – or not. The key concern is the contribution margin associated with the average product sale. *Contribution margin* is sales minus all variable expenses, and can be calculated from the income statement. In the following portion of a sample income statement, we extract the costs of materials and labor from the cost of goods sold, and subtract them from sales to arrive at the average contribution margin. The relevant portions of the income statement are noted in bold.

Sample Derivation of Contribution Margin

Sales		**$1,000,000**
Cost of goods sold:		
Direct materials	**$250,000**	
Direct labor	**80,000**	
Factory overhead	190,000	
Total cost of goods sold		$520,000
Contribution margin	**670,000**	
Contribution margin percentage	**67%**	
Gross margin		$480,000
Gross margin percentage		48%

Because factory overhead is a fixed cost, we exclude it from the contribution margin calculation. The result is typically quite a high contribution margin percentage. This is of some importance when matched with the amount of accounts receivable outstanding, for it indicates the proportion of cash that a business actually has invested in its accounts receivable.

For example, if a business has a high average contribution margin, it generates a high profit margin with each sale, and so has little cash invested in each receivable. This means it can afford to extend quite generous payment terms to its customers without investing much cash in the resulting receivables. For this type of business, a relatively high bad debt percentage may be inconsequential, since the bad debt can be easily offset by the large profits, and the company loses little cash when a receivable is written off.

The situation is entirely different when the contribution margin is quite small. In this case, a business cannot afford to have any bad debt, and so will tightly restrict the extension of credit to only its best customers. If a receivable cannot be collected, then nearly the entire amount of the receivable represents lost cash that the business cannot recover.

Relative Importance of Inventory

In some industries, the proper management of inventory is a key driver of profitability, and so is closely watched by investors. In other industries, inventory is a complete nonevent, since its use has little impact on sales. Given this wide range of outcomes, you should first review the industry within which a business operates, as well as its specific competitive stance, to determine the extent to which inventory is a concern. Here are several examples of how inventory can impact a business:

Industry

- *Services industries*. There are many industries where there is no inventory at all, or where it comprises a vanishingly small proportion of sales. In these industries, the emphasis is more likely to be on the delivery of personal services – for example, to provide consulting, tax advice, or perhaps field service to faulty equipment. If any inventory is kept on hand, it is probably for very specific and high-margin uses, such as maintaining a store of key repair parts for the copier machines of clients.
- *Hospitality industry*. This industry is comprised of hotels, restaurants, spas, casinos, and similar businesses. Their main type of inventory is the ingredients for meals; since this inventory tends to spoil quickly, there is a self-regulating feature that forces a business to use inventory or throw it out, resulting in very high inventory usage rates. There may also be a small amount of merchandise sales, such as workout clothes sold by spas, but the amount of these sales is incidental to operations.
- *Clothing industry*. The customers of clothing designers are fickle in the extreme, so new designs must be brought to market quickly and inventory levels monitored daily to guard against sudden declines in demand. Excess stocks

may be unloaded to discounters once demand drops off to a sufficient extent. In this industry, constant inventory monitoring is mandatory.

- *Repair parts*. Customers may require replacement parts for all sorts of equipment, and may continue to require them for many years after the original equipment purchase. Examples are repair parts for vehicles, washers and dryers, and air conditioning units. In the repair business, inventory may be stored for years before it is sold, but can then be sold at very high margins. Consequently, there is an incentive to initially keep fairly high inventory levels, after which a key concern is watching demand over time to decide whether any of the residual inventory levels can be considered obsolete. This can be quite a difficult inventory management environment.

The presented industries are intended to provide examples of the differing impacts of inventory on a business, ranging from none at all in the services business to high turnover levels in the hospitality and clothing industries, to low turnover levels in the repair parts business.

Competitive Stance

- *Low-cost model*. A business may choose to compete by keeping the cost of its products low, so that it can pass these savings along to customers through low prices. To do so, it is necessary to minimize unit costs by such means as highly efficient production systems and lengthy production runs. Under this approach, you should look for medium-to-high inventory levels in proportion to sales.
- *High service model*. The reverse of the low-cost model is to charge a higher price in return for excellent service. This means keeping extra inventory on hand, so that orders can be filled at once. When this model is being used, it is especially critical to monitor inventory levels, since it is quite possible that too much inventory will be kept in stock, which absorbs cash and can trigger losses due to obsolete inventory.
- *Full product range model*. A marketing-driven company can elect to offer many models of its products, so that every possible customer niche is addressed. While great from a sales perspective, this approach requires a business to maintain inventory for every variation of product that it sells. This model calls for constant attention to inventory balances, since there is a risk of having too much old inventory for which there is no demand.
- *Retail model*. A retailer must maintain adequate stocks of inventory, or else its shelves will appear to be barren, and its customer traffic will decline. Consequently, these operations require significant inventory levels, as well as constant sales monitoring to see if any inventory should be sold off to discounters.
- *Internet store pass-through model*. A common inventory management technique used by some Internet stores is to set rock-bottom prices, take money in advance from customers, and then order the required inventory items from

their suppliers. This means that customers wait a long time for delivery, but the store operators maintain essentially no inventory.

Of the competitive models just described, those that bear the most watching are the high service model and the full product range model, where it is easy for a non-observant management team to let inventory levels skyrocket, soaking up excess cash and increasing the risk of inventory write-offs.

Sufficiency of Depreciation

From the perspective of long-term competitiveness, a business should be investing roughly the same amount in new fixed assets over time, to replace its old assets as they gradually wear out. It is possible to estimate the amount of this asset replacement by examining the proportion of depreciation to gross fixed assets over time. The proportion should remain roughly the same, especially when the straight-line method of depreciation is being used (since it does not accelerate depreciation charges). The concept is expanded upon in the following example.

EXAMPLE

An investor is reviewing the financial statements of Hodgson Industrial Design, which uses stamping machines to create large numbers of aluminum widgets. The stamping machines wear out after about ten years of continuous use, and must then be replaced. Hodgson's management team has been attempting to aggressively expand the sale of its widgets into the South American market, which has called for a delicate balancing act of investing in more equipment without taking on too much debt. She extracts the following information from Hodgson's balance sheets for the past four years. The expansion began in Year 3.

(000s)	Year 1	Year 2	Year 3	Year 4
Gross fixed assets	$18,500	$18,900	$23,400	$25,100
Net change in accumulated depreciation	2,002	2,079	2,106	1,757
Net change in accumulated depreciation as % of gross fixed assets	11%	11%	9%	7%

The table reveals that there is an increase in the overall investment in fixed assets, as one would expect to see when sales are increasing rapidly. However, the proportion of depreciation to gross fixed assets has declined, which indicates that Hodgson's management is probably retaining an increasing proportion of old and fully depreciated stamping machines. A likely outcome is that a number of machines will need to be replaced in the near future, when they completely wear out. Another possible outcome is that some machines will fail suddenly, resulting in the company's inability to meet its sales commitments.

There can be valid reasons for a declining proportion of depreciation to gross fixed assets. Here are several possible scenarios:

- *Outsourcing*. A company may have chosen to outsource some or all of its production capabilities to a third party, which allows it to sell off its production assets.
- *Bottleneck focus*. Management may have decided to focus its attention on enhancing the ability of the business to utilize its bottleneck operation. If so, there is less inclination to over-invest in other parts of the business.
- *Life extension*. It is possible to extend the useful life of equipment through the use of preventive maintenance and periodic overhauls. This means the equipment can continue to be used past the point when it has been fully depreciated.

There are also valid reasons for an *increasing* proportion of depreciation to gross fixed assets. Here are several possible scenarios:

- *Bottleneck support*. Management may have decided to invest in more fixed assets upstream from the bottleneck operation in the production area. This is called *sprint capacity*, and is intended to provide a boost in production volume following an unexpected production stoppage. Having extra sprint capacity allows a bottleneck operation to continue operating at full capacity. See the author's *Constraint Management* course for more information.
- *Competitive change*. Management may have decided to increase the investment in certain fixed assets in order to give the company a competitive advantage, perhaps to customize products to the needs of individual customers, or to lower costs. This approach can involve such a large increase in the fixed asset investment that it poses a barrier to entry for potential new competitors.
- *Reduced useful life*. Management may have decided that the existing fixed assets will have a shorter life than was originally anticipated, so the periodic amount of depreciation recognized increases to ensure that it is fully recognized by the end of the shortened useful life.

Proportion of Sales to Fixed Assets

It requires a large amount of fixed assets to compete in some industries, such as computer chips and automobiles. The sales to fixed assets ratio can be used to determine how a company's expenditures for fixed assets compare to those of other companies in the same industry, to see if it is operating in a more lean fashion than the others, or if there may be opportunities to scale back on its fixed asset investment. This is quite useful to track on a trend line, which may show gradual changes in expenditure levels away from the historical trend. The ratio is most useful in asset-intensive industries, and least useful when the required asset base is so small that the ratio would be essentially meaningless.

The ratio can also be misleading in cases when a company must invest in an entire production facility before it can generate any sales; this will initially result in an inordinately low sales to fixed assets ratio, which gradually increases as the company maximizes sales for that facility, and then levels out when it reaches a high level of asset utilization.

To calculate the sales to fixed assets ratio, divide net sales for the past twelve months by the book value of all fixed assets. Book value is the recognized fixed asset cost, minus accumulated depreciation. The formula is:

$$\frac{\text{Trailing 12 months' sales}}{\text{Book value of all fixed assets}}$$

The fixed asset book value listed in the denominator is subject to some variation, depending on what type of depreciation method is used. If an accelerated depreciation method is used, the denominator will be unusually small, and so will yield a higher ratio.

EXAMPLE

Mole Industries manufactures trench digging equipment. It has a relatively low sales to fixed assets ratio of 4:1, because a large amount of machining equipment is needed to construct its products. Mole is considering expanding into earth-moving equipment, and calculates the sales to fixed assets ratio for competing companies, based on their financial statements. The ratio is in the vicinity of 3:1 for most competitors, which means that Mole will need to invest heavily in fixed assets in order to enter this new market. Mole estimates that the most likely revenue level it can achieve for earth moving equipment will be $300 million. Based on the 3:1 ratio, this means that Mole may need to invest $100 million in fixed assets in order to achieve its goal.

Days Payables Outstanding

The accounts payable days formula measures the number of days that a company takes to pay its suppliers. If the number of days increases from one period to the next, this indicates that the company is paying its suppliers more slowly.

To calculate days payables outstanding, summarize all purchases from suppliers during the measurement period, and divide by the average amount of accounts payable during that period. The formula is:

$$\frac{\text{Total supplier purchases}}{(\text{Beginning accounts payable} + \text{Ending accounts payable}) \div 2}$$

This formula reveals the total accounts payable turnover. Then divide the resulting turnover figure into 365 days to arrive at the number of accounts payable days.

The formula can be modified to exclude cash payments to suppliers, since the numerator should include only purchases on credit from suppliers. However, the amount of up-front cash payments to suppliers is normally so small that this modification is not necessary.

As an example, an investor wants to determine a company's accounts payable days for the past year. In the beginning of this period, the beginning accounts payable

81

balance was $800,000, and the ending balance was $884,000. Purchases for the last 12 months were $7,500,000. Based on this information, the accounts payable turnover calculation is:

$$\frac{\$7,500,000 \text{ Purchases}}{(\$800,000 \text{ Beginning payables} + \$884,000 \text{ Ending payables}) \div 2}$$

$$=$$

$$\frac{\$7,500,000 \text{ Purchases}}{\$842,000 \text{ Average accounts payable}}$$

$$= 8.9 \text{ Accounts payable turnover}$$

Thus, the company's accounts payable is turning over at a rate of 8.9 times per year. To calculate the turnover in days, divide the 8.9 turns into 365 days, which yields:

$$365 \text{ Days} \div 8.9 \text{ Turns} = 41 \text{ Days}$$

One might measure accounts payable days by only using the cost of goods sold in the numerator. This is incorrect, since there may be a large amount of administrative expenses that should also be included. If only the cost of goods sold is included in the numerator, this creates an excessively small number of payable days.

A significant failing of the days payables outstanding measurement is that it does not factor in all of the short-term liabilities of a business. There may be substantial liabilities related to payroll, interest, and taxes that exceed the size of payables outstanding. This issue can be eliminated by incorporating all short-term liabilities into the days payables outstanding measurement.

Changes in Payable Days

The number of payable days should be fairly consistent from one period to the next, since it is largely based on the payment terms of suppliers, which change infrequently. There is typically a mix of payment terms among suppliers, such as 30-day terms for raw material suppliers and 10-day terms for freight companies. As long as the mix of these suppliers is consistent, the aggregate payable days should not change. Also, even if the sales volume of a business spikes or drops, the payable days should remain about the same. If there is a change, here are several possibilities for why the change has occurred:

Decline in Payable Days

- *Tighter credit policy.* Suppliers may have tightened their credit policies, which either allows a company to have less total credit with them or requires them to pay sooner. This circumstance can arise when the economy is contracting, but is more likely if a business has abused its payment terms in the past. The latter scenario is more likely if payable days contracts substantially, since it implies that suppliers are requiring cash on delivery terms.

- *Large invoice paid.* The company may have just paid quite a large invoice amount, which comprises a large part of the total accounts payable. This condition is more likely in a small business that has few suppliers, but could also arise when a department has been outsourced, and large periodic payments are due to the supplier that has taken over this function.
- *Early payment discounts taken.* If a business has a large store of excess cash on hand, one profitable use for it is to take all possible early payment discounts offered by suppliers, especially since the effective interest rate offered by suppliers is usually quite high. This is likely to be the case when a business has an unusually high cash or investments balance.

Increase in Payable Days

- *Change in payment terms.* An aggressive purchasing department could negotiate for longer payment terms with suppliers. This is most likely to be the case for large companies that make large purchases from suppliers, and so can demand favorable terms. A smaller company does not have the purchasing power to force through longer payment terms, and so could probably only do so in exchange for paying more per unit; if so, the increased cost will appear in the cost of goods sold.
- *Intentionally delayed payments.* The controller may not have sufficient cash to pay supplier invoices on time, and so delays making payments. Evidence of this situation is when the cash balance is persistently low and the available line of credit has been fully accessed.

Financial Leverage

Financial leverage is the amount of debt that an entity uses to buy more assets. This is done to avoid investing an organization's own equity capital in such purchases.

The financial leverage formula is measured as the ratio of total debt to total assets. As the proportion of debt to assets increases, so too does the amount of financial leverage. Financial leverage is favorable when the uses to which debt can be put generate returns greater than the interest expense associated with the debt. Many companies use financial leverage rather than acquiring more equity capital, which could reduce the earnings per share of existing shareholders. Financial leverage has two primary advantages:

- *Enhanced earnings.* Financial leverage may allow an entity to earn a disproportionate amount on its assets.
- *Favorable tax treatment.* In many tax jurisdictions, interest expense is tax deductible, which reduces its net cost to the borrower.

However, financial leverage also presents the possibility of disproportionate losses, since the related amount of interest expense may overwhelm the borrower if it does not earn sufficient returns to offset the interest expense. This is a particular problem when interest rates rise or the returns from assets decline.

Financial leverage is an especially risky approach in a cyclical business, or one in which there are low barriers to entry, since sales and profits are more likely to fluctuate considerably from year to year, increasing the risk of bankruptcy over time. Conversely, financial leverage may be an acceptable alternative when a company is located in an industry with steady revenue levels, large cash reserves, and high barriers to entry, since operating conditions are sufficiently steady to support a large amount of leverage with little downside.

There is usually a natural limitation on the amount of financial leverage, since lenders are less likely to forward additional funds to a borrower that has already borrowed a large amount of debt.

In short, financial leverage can earn outsized returns for shareholders, but also presents the risk of outright bankruptcy if cash flows fall below expectations.

EXAMPLE

Able Company uses $1,000,000 of its own cash to buy a factory, which generates $150,000 of annual profits. The company is not using financial leverage at all, since it incurred no debt to buy the factory.

Baker Company uses $100,000 of its own cash and a loan of $900,000 to buy a similar factory, which also generates a $150,000 annual profit. Baker is using financial leverage to generate a profit of $150,000 on a cash investment of $100,000, which is a 150% return on its investment.

Baker's new factory has a bad year, and generates a loss of $300,000, which is triple the amount of its original investment.

Relative Size of Debt

When can the amount of the debt obligations of a business be considered minor? There is no consistent rule, since fluctuations in any company's business model can cut into its ability to repay debt. Nonetheless, here are several indicators that the relative amount of debt held is not a concern:

- The amount of cash and investments held exceeds the amount of debt. This implies that a company could theoretically pay off its debt from current reserves.
- The amount of reported annual net income could pay off the debt within a few years. This concept assumes that cash flows roughly equate to the reported profitability level, which is not necessarily the case.

The Book Value Concept

The *book value* of a business is the amount of assets stated on its balance sheet, minus the liabilities listed on the balance sheet. Or, stated as a formula, book value is:

$$Assets - Liabilities = Book\ value$$

Book value is a commonly-used measure of the value of a business, probably because it is so easily derived from the published balance sheet of a company. The information could be used to estimate the most appropriate price of a company's stock, such as by comparing the market price of the stock to its book value. Or, the book value concept could be one possible basis for deriving the value of a company, when a potential acquirer wants to issue a bid to the owners of the target company. Also, lenders commonly use book value to estimate whether a prospective or current borrower is a good credit risk. In short, book value has many possible uses.

Despite the widespread use of book value, it is a seriously flawed measurement. The problem is that the amounts stated in a company's balance sheet do not necessarily match their current market values. Instead, some are recorded at their original purchase prices, while others are adjusted to their market values as of the balance sheet date. The problem is exacerbated by the Generally Accepted Accounting Principles (GAAP) framework, which enforces the recordation of the most conservative values for assets. The issue is less of a problem if the International Financial Reporting Standards (IFRS) framework is used, since IFRS allows for the upward revaluation of some assets.

A further issue with book value is the incorporation of intangible assets into the balance sheet. An *intangible asset* is a non-physical asset that has a useful life spanning more than one accounting period. Examples of intangible assets are software developed for internal use, patents, and copyrights. If a company internally generates intangible assets, the business cannot usually record these assets on its balance sheet. In some cases, the value of these assets represents the primary value of an entire business, so the book value calculation may wildly underestimate the value of the organization.

Conversely, an acquirer is allowed to record that portion of the purchase price of an acquiree that can be allocated to the intangible assets of the acquiree. For example, a portion of the purchase price may be allocated to an intangible asset called "customer relationships," which is then amortized over the presumed remaining life of those relationships. In some cases, these intangible assets can be considered specious at best, and yet are included in the book value calculation because they are listed on the balance sheet.

A further problem with acquisitions is that any portion of the purchase price that cannot be allocated to tangible or intangible assets is recorded as "goodwill," which appears in the balance sheet as an asset. In some cases, goodwill can represent a large part of the assets listed on a company's balance sheet, and so can radically skew the calculation of book value.

For the reasons enumerated here, we do not recommend using the book value concept for the purposes of assigning a value to an entire business. The value derived would be nearly arbitrary, and could bear little relationship to the actual market value of the entity.

Book Value per Share

The primary user of book value is the investor, who wants to compare the market value of shares owned to their book value, and so needs a measurement that is presented on a per-share basis.

The measurement is typically calculated on the basis of just common stock, with the effects of preferred stock eliminated from the calculation. By doing so, the result shows the amount that a common shareholder might receive upon the liquidation of a business.

To calculate book value per share, subtract preferred stock from stockholders' equity and divide by the number of common shares outstanding. Be sure to use the average number of shares in the denominator, since the period-end amount may incorporate a recent stock buyback or issuance, and so could skew the results. The formula is:

(Stockholders' equity – Preferred stock) ÷ Average common shares = Book value per share

---

EXAMPLE

Grissom Granaries has $15,000,000 of stockholders' equity, $3,000,000 of preferred stock, and an average of 2,000,000 shares outstanding during the measurement period. The calculation of its book value per share is:

$$\frac{\$15,000,000 \text{ Stockholders' equity} - \$3,000,000 \text{ Preferred stock}}{2,000,000 \text{ Average common shares outstanding}}$$

$$= \$6.00 \text{ Book value per share}$$

Interpreting the Income Statement

The *income statement* contains the results of an organization's operations for a specific period of time, showing revenues and expenses and the resulting profit or loss. The typical period covered by an income statement is for a month, quarter, or year, though it could cover just a few days.

An income statement is used to measure the ability of an organization to achieve sales, and its efficiency in servicing customers. If a business does well in both respects, then it earns a profit. A profit is the amount by which sales exceed expenses. Instead, if expenses exceed sales, then the entity generates a loss. The cumulative amount of this profit or loss, net of any dividends paid to investors, appears in the retained earnings line item in the balance sheet.

The basic format of an income statement is noted in the following exhibit. It contains a header, which describes the name of the entity whose financial information is being reported on, the name of the report, and the date range for which information is being presented. In the following line items, we have noted how each one adds up into the various subtotals and totals in the document. The flow of information in the statement is to begin at the top with sales, subtract out expenses directly related to sales, then subtract all other expenses to arrive at before-tax income, and then subtract income taxes to arrive at the net income figure.

Sample Income Statement Format

Laid Back Corporation
Income Statement
For the month ended December 31, 20X1

Net sales	A
Cost of goods sold	B
Gross margin	A – B = C
Operating expenses	
Advertising	D
Depreciation	E
Rent	F
Payroll taxes	G
Salaries and wages	H
Supplies	I
Travel and entertainment	J
Total operating expenses	D + E + F + G + H + I + J = K
Other income	L
Total income before taxes	C – K + L = M
Income taxes	N
Net income	M - N

To see how these calculations are used in an income statement, the following example replaces the line item computations with numbers taken from the general ledger of a business.

Sample Income Statement with Numeric Presentation

Laid Back Corporation
Income Statement
For the month ended December 31, 20X1

Net sales	$1,000,000
Cost of goods sold	480,000
Gross margin	$520,000
Operating expenses	
Advertising	10,000
Depreciation	8,000
Rent	32,000
Payroll taxes	25,000
Salaries and wages	359,000
Supplies	5,000
Travel and entertainment	11,000
Total operating expenses	$450,000
Other income	10,000
Total income before taxes	$80,000
Income taxes	30,000
Net income	050,000

In short, the balance sheet provides a point-in-time picture of a business, while the income statement provides a report card on its results in between these point-in-time snapshots.

The Trend of Sales

When a company has just been founded, its percentage growth rate may be astounding, as the entity fills its primary market niche. Once the niche is filled, management will likely resort to a number of strategies to expand sales, but the rate of sales growth will decline. At some point, it is possible that new competition or entirely new product categories will put pressure on price points and reduce customer demand, resulting in a decline in sales. The following table shows a sample of how to determine the ongoing trend of sales.

Sample Sales Trend Analysis

(000s)	Year 1	Year 2	Year 3	Year 4	Year 5	Year 6
Sales	$1,000	$1,800	$2,400	$2,900	$3,200	$3,100
Sales $ change	--	$800	$600	$500	$300	-$100
Sales % change*		**80%**	**33%**	**21%**	**10%**	**-3%**

* The calculation is the increase over the past year's sales, divided by the past year's sales

In the sample trend analysis, the initially massive growth rate ends after the second year, with a continually declining growth rate through the fifth year. Sales then begin to decline. The trend is not always this clear, but a pattern can usually be observed.

A variation on sales trend analysis is same-store sales, which is information that a retail business may publish along with its financial statements. Investors like to watch the sales growth in stores that have already been open for at least a year, to see if a company's products, marketing efforts, and price management can continue to attract an increasing growth pattern.

A rapid rate of sales growth will attract the attention of growth-oriented investors, who want to profit from a surging stock price. Once the sales trend backs away from its initial levels, management may change from its initial focus on sales growth and be more focused on cash flow and profitability. At this point, the initial group of growth-oriented investors will be replaced by income-oriented investors who are more interested in the regularity of cash flows provided by ongoing dividend payments. If there is a sales decline, the stock price will likely drop, which will attract the attention of value investors who want to buy shares at a low price, in hopes of a later resurgence in the stock price.

In short, all of the preceding types of investors closely watch the trend of sales, since the rate of growth (or decline) drives their investment strategies.

The Quality of Sales

There is ongoing pressure on a business to continually increase its sales, in order to expand the return to investors. This can be a problem when a company eventually maximizes its initial target market. At that point, management may take several steps to add on more sales, such as offering credit to new customers who have questionable payment histories, selling add-on accessories or services (such as product warranties), entering entirely new market niches, or selling in new geographic regions. Each of these decisions can result in sales that are of differing levels of quality. Quality can be defined in many ways, but from the viewpoint of analyzing sales, our focus is on the profit margin associated with each incremental sale. Thus, a high-quality sale carries with it a high profit margin.

This issue is a major concern to the outside reviewer, who has no idea if the next tranche of sales will come from a new group of customers, products, or regions. Here are several indicators that the quality of sales may be declining:

- *Bad debt increases.* If the bad debt expense suddenly increases, it may mean that management has decided to grant credit to a new group of lower-quality customers, in a bid to expand sales. This likely means that the bad debt expense is layered on top of the existing product margins, resulting in an overall reduction in the profitability percentage.

- *Commission increase.* When a company opens up a new sales region, it may offer unusually high sales commissions to its sales staff in order to develop the region. This issue can be detected by calculating the commission expense as a percentage of sales on a trend line.
- *Distribution costs increase.* If the cost of distributing products is broken out on the income statement, a jump in this expense may indicate that a company is expanding its warehousing and retail operations into new geographic regions. If these regions have a lower population per square mile than the company's existing sales regions, the result could be an increased distribution cost per sale, which reduces the profitability percentage.
- *Cost of sales increase.* If there is a sharp increase in the cost of goods sold, there is a good chance that management elected to reduce product prices in order to spur sales. If the cost increase only occurs once, it is possible that management conducted a one-time sale to eliminate older items from inventory.

The preceding points do not necessarily mean that a business will begin to incur losses as it pursues more sales – only that some additional costs will be incurred that will reduce the profit percentage that is earned. If losses *are* being incurred as sales increase, then one must question management's ability to identify which tranche of sales is causing the problem, and to correct the issue.

The Reliability of Sales

Investors tend to place a higher valuation on a business that has highly reliable sales. We define reliability as sales that are highly likely to recur. For example, a business that sells subscriptions to its services (such as cell phone plans) can be considered to have reliable sales. Also, a business that is in a monopoly position (such as a power company) reports reliable sales, since customers have no choice other than to buy its services. It can be quite difficult to discern which types of company sales are more reliable, unless the entity decides to report different types of sales in separate line items in its income statement. It is also possible that types of sales will be broken out in more detail in the accompanying footnotes.

Gross Margin Analysis

The gross profit ratio shows the proportion of profits generated by the sale of goods or services, before operating expenses. In essence, it reveals the ability of a business to create sellable products in a cost-effective manner. The ratio is of some importance from an analysis perspective, especially when tracked on a trend line, to see if a business is continuing to provide products to the marketplace for which customers are willing to pay.

The ratio can also be used for comparison to the gross margins of competitors. When a business' gross margin is unusually low, it could mean that management is cutting prices in order to remain competitive. This situation is most likely when the organization is a small one, and is competing against larger national entities that have obvious cost efficiencies.

The gross profit ratio is calculated as sales minus the cost of goods sold, divided by sales. The formula is:

$$\frac{\text{Sales} - \text{Cost of goods sold}}{\text{Sales}}$$

The ratio can vary over time as sales volumes change, since the cost of goods sold contains some fixed cost elements that will not vary with sales volume.

EXAMPLE

An investor is reviewing the gross profit ratio for Quest Adventure Gear, which includes financial statements for the past three years. The investor extracts the following information from the financial statements of Quest:

	20X1	20X2	20X3
Sales	$12,000,000	$13,500,000	$14,800,000
Cost of goods sold	5,040,000	6,075,000	7,252,000
Gross profit ratio	58%	55%	51%

The analysis reveals that Quest is suffering from an ongoing decline in its gross profits, which should certainly be a concern for the investor.

An organization may be showing signs of trying to improve its gross margin percentage. There are a number of ways to do so, including the following:

- Outsourcing production
- Stripping away excess production capacity
- Upgrading to more efficient production equipment
- Centralizing purchases with a smaller number of suppliers, to gain volume discounts
- Redesigning products to reduce the cost of raw materials and the production process
- Layoffs of production staff
- Raising prices

The Inventory Build Concept

If a company operates in a highly seasonal industry (such as snow blowers, ski equipment, or patio furniture), it will likely need to begin the production of goods well before customers begin to place orders. This means that all production costs will be absorbed into inventory during the no-sales months, with no cost of goods sold appearing in the income statement at all until deliveries are sent to customers. During the period when there are no sales, the income statement will present no sales, cost of goods sold, or gross margin. Instead, the inventory line item in the balance sheet will store the production costs incurred during that period.

Strategy Impact on Operating Expenses

When management decides to follow the strategy of keeping prices low in order to gain market share, this usually means cutting deeply into operating expenses, too. For example, the marketing budget could be skimpy, while the research and development budget could be ranked among the lowest in the industry. In addition, the corporate structure is more likely to be flat, so that fewer managers are needed. The end result is a set of operating expenses that are decidedly low in relation to those of competitors.

At the opposite end of the spectrum is a business that emphasizes full service and/or customization. In this case, high prices are the norm, which need to be justified with a plush marketing budget, excellent customer service, and a well-funded research staff.

Neither approach presented here can be considered better than the other – they must instead be viewed in terms of the overall competitive stance that management has adopted for the entire business.

From a stock investment perspective, companies that invest large sums in research and development tend to experience large swings in their stock prices, depending on the outcome of their research activities. The investor who is willing to tolerate the riskiness of these price swings could earn a fortune if a major new product is released, or suffer an equally large loss if a new product introduction fails. Thus, the risk-averse investor might want to consider industries in which research and development spending tends to be low.

Effects of Interest Expense

The chief element of the other income section of the income statement is usually interest expense. This is considered a financing cost, so it is not included in the operating expenses section of the income statement. The amount of this expense is mainly based on management's decisions regarding how fast to grow the business and whether this growth should be funded with debt. In a high-growth situation, it will be necessary to invest in much more working capital and more fixed assets. If there is an unwillingness to sell more shares, or if lenders are willing to loan money at low rates, the outcome may be a large amount of debt, for which there will be a correspondingly large interest expense.

If a business is a small one, it will be less likely to obtain cheap financing, and will instead have to resort to high-cost lending arrangements, such as the factoring of receivables. Consequently, if the implicit interest rate associated with debt is quite high, you can reasonably infer that management is being forced into very high-cost borrowing arrangements. This is a particular problem when the before-tax profit margin is already low, since a business probably cannot afford the cost of debt.

Net Profit Margin

The net profit margin is a comparison of after-tax income to net sales[2]. It reveals the remaining income after all costs of production and operations have been deducted from sales, and income taxes recognized. As such, it is a reasonable measure of the overall results of a firm, especially when combined with an evaluation of how well it is using its working capital. The measure is commonly reported on a trend line, to judge performance over time. It is also used to compare the results of a business with its competitors.

The net profit margin is really a short-term measurement, because it does not reveal a company's actions to maintain profitability over the long term, as may be indicated by the level of capital investment or research and development expenditures. Also, a company may delay a variety of discretionary expenses, such as maintenance or training, to make its net profit margin look better than it normally is. Consequently, evaluate this margin alongside an array of other metrics to gain a better picture of a company's ability to continue as a going concern.

Another issue with the net profit margin is that a company may intentionally keep it low through a variety of expense recognition strategies in order to avoid paying taxes. If so, review the statement of cash flows to determine the real cash-generating ability of a business.

To calculate the net profit margin, divide net profits by net sales and then multiply by 100. The formula is:

$$(\text{Net profit} \div \text{Net sales}) \times 100$$

EXAMPLE

Kelvin Corporation has $1,000,000 of sales in its most recent month, as well as sales returns of $40,000, a cost of goods sold of $550,000, and operating expenses of $360,000. The income tax rate is 35%. The calculation of its net profit margin is:

$1,000,000 Sales - $40,000 Sales returns = $960,000 Net sales

$960,000 Net sales - $550,000 Cost of goods - $360,000 Operating expenses

= $50,000 Income before tax

---

[2] Net sales is gross sales minus sales discounts.

$50,000 Income before tax $\times (1 - 0.35) = \underline{\$32,500 \text{ Profit after tax}}$

($32,500 Profit after tax $\div$ $960,000 Net Sales) $\times$ 100

= 3.4% Net profit margin

The Big Bath

Another expense issue to be aware of is the *big bath*. This is a large one-time write-off that management elects to take, usually in the form of a large reserve. By setting up this reserve, they can then take charges in the future that offset the reserve. The reason for taking a big bath is to completely obliterate profits in the current period in order to make future periods look more profitable. Taking a big bath is most common in periods when management knows the company will already be generating poor earnings, so the thinking is to get the poor earnings report out of the way all at once.

This approach is generally legal, but it has a reputation for being used too much to manipulate earnings – sometimes for several years into the future. You should be especially suspicious when the reporting entity has a history of repeatedly recording a big bath every few years, after which it reports unusually strong earnings – until the next big bath.

Management may also elect to take a big bath when it wants to write off assets that are currently recorded at fraudulently-high levels or which have been inadequately depreciated. As an example, a manager might create fake sales, which requires a matching fake customer billing. A big bath can then be used to write off this billing before anyone investigates why it has not been paid.

Another use for a big bath is when management wants to earn bonus payments in later years. They report a big bath in losing years when they have no chance of earning a bonus, thereby enhancing the chance that they will earn bonuses in later periods, when they can charge expenses to the big bath reserve, thereby driving up profits.

You should be especially watchful for big bath reporting in public companies, since they are more focused on presenting highly favorable earnings information to the investment community.

Interpreting the Statement of Cash Flows

The *statement of cash flows* is used to identify the different types of cash payments made by a business to third parties (cash outflows), as well as payments made to a business by third parties (cash inflows). Though less frequently used than the balance sheet and income statement, this additional report provides valuable information about the cash status of a business.

This statement is needed, because the information in the income statement does not exactly correspond to cash flows. Instead, an accrual-basis income statement may record revenues and expenses for which cash flows have not yet occurred. In addition, there is no information in the income statement regarding the cash required to support investments in receivables, fixed assets, inventory, and other assets, nor is there any information about cash flows related to the sale of stock, obtaining or paying back loans, and similar matters.

The basic format of a statement of cash flows is noted in the following exhibit. It contains a header, which describes the name of the entity whose financial information is being reported on, the name of the report, and the date range for which information is being presented. In the following line items, we have noted how each one adds up into the various subtotals and totals in the document. The flow of information in the statement is to begin with a derivation of cash flows generated by the operations of a business, followed by the cash flows associated with investing activities and financing activities, which results in a net change in cash for the period. Cash flows are separated into the operating, investing, and financing activities classifications in order to give the reader more information about how cash is generated and used.

Sample Statement of Cash Flows Format

Newton Enterprises
Statement of Cash Flows
For the year ended 12/31/20X1

Cash flows from operating activities		
Net income		A
Adjustments for:		
Depreciation and amortization	B	
Provision for losses on accounts receivable	C	
Gain/loss on sale of assets	D	
		B + C + D = E
Increase/decrease in accounts receivables	F	
Increase/decrease in inventories	G	
Increase/decrease in trade payables	H	
		F + G + H = I
Cash generated from/used in operations		A + E + I = J
Cash flows from investing activities		
Purchase of fixed assets	K	
Proceeds from sale of equipment	L	
Net cash generated from/used in investing activities		K + L = M
Cash flows from financing activities		
Proceeds from issuance of common stock	N	
Proceeds from issuance of long-term debt	O	
Dividends paid	P	
Net cash generated from/used in financing activities		N + O + P = Q
Net increase/decrease in cash and cash equivalents		J + M + Q = R
Cash and cash equivalents at beginning of period		S
Cash and cash equivalents at end of period		R + S

To see how these calculations are used in a statement of cash flows, the following example replaces the line item computations with numbers taken from the general ledger of a business.

Sample Statement of Cash Flows with Numeric Presentation

Newton Enterprises
Statement of Cash Flows
For the year ended 12/31/20X1

Cash flows from operating activities		
Net income		$100,000
Adjustments for:		
Depreciation and amortization	12,000	
Provision for losses on accounts receivable	18,000	
Gain on sale of assets	-10,000	
		20,000
Increase in accounts receivables	-80,000	
Decrease in inventories	30,000	
Decrease in trade payables	-16,000	
		-66,000
Cash generated from operations		54,000
Cash flows from investing activities		
Purchase of fixed assets	-80,000	
Proceeds from sale of equipment	24,000	
Net cash used in investing activities		-56,000
Cash flows from financing activities		
Proceeds from issuance of common stock	120,000	
Proceeds from issuance of long-term debt	57,000	
Dividends paid	-32,000	
Cash generated from financing activities		145,000
Net increase in cash and cash equivalents		143,000
Cash and cash equivalents at beginning of period		230,000
Cash and cash equivalents at end of period		$373,000

Some elements of the statement of cash flows are derived from the other financial statements. The net income figure comes from the income statement, along with several of the net income adjustment items. The cash balances at the bottom of the report are taken from the balance sheet, while the increases and decreases in the various assets and liabilities are derived by calculating the differences between the line items in the most recent balance sheet and the same line items in the balance sheet pertaining to the end of the immediately preceding reporting period. For example, the change in accounts receivable noted in the statement of cash flows is derived by calculating the difference in the accounts receivable line items in the last two balance sheets.

Examination of Cash Flows from Operating Activities

An issue with the cash flows from operating activities section is that the information is summarized at quite a high level. This means it can be difficult to extract information from it. Nonetheless, here are several areas to examine:

- *Cash generated from operations.* The single easiest item to monitor is the total cash generated from operations. Monitor this item on a trend line to see if there are consistently positive cash flows. Also, put in an adjacent trend line the reported operating profit of the business. Operating profit is the gross profit minus all operating expenses, but before the effects of other income and taxes. If there is a large and ongoing disparity between the two trend lines, a deeper investigation may be warranted, as noted in the following example.

EXAMPLE

An investor is reviewing the financial statements of Geodetic International. The company has two divisions. One consistently generates profits from the hourly billing of the federal government for the conversion of wildfire information into maps. The other division is developing an internal software package that will automatically convert satellite imagery into soil maps. A selection of Geodetic's reported financial information is as follows:

(000s)	Year 1	Year 2	Year 3	Year 4
Operating profit	$1,000	$1,200	$1,700	$2,000
Cash generated from operations	-200	-300	-300	-300
Disparity	-1,200	-1,500	-2,000	-2,300
Cash balance	500	--	--	--
Change in fixed assets	+1,400	+1,700	+2,200	+2,500
Change in short-term loans	+900	+1,700	+2,200	+2,500

The evidence strongly indicates that Geodetic's management is capitalizing the software development cost associated with its new satellite imagery software. The full amount of the disparity between the reported operating profit and the cash generated from operations is being shifted into the fixed assets line item in the balance sheet and being funded with short-term debt. The result is a highly misleading income statement, as well as a dangerous increase in short-term debt, which is subject to short-term interest rate fluctuations.

- *Change in working capital elements.* A good place to view changes in the various elements of working capital is in this section. The specific changes in trade receivables, inventories, and payables are noted. When individually tracked on a trend line, it is possible to see where a business is investing its working capital funds.

EXAMPLE

The management of Ninja Cutlery is engaged in a rapid expansion of its ceramic knife business from the professional chef market to home cooks. The trouble is that reaching home cooks requires distributing through several retail chains, which require long payment terms. The outcome of this new direction for the company appears in the following working capital figures, which were extracted from its statement of cash flows. Sales into the new market began in the second quarter.

(000s)	Quarter 1	Quarter 2	Quarter 3	Quarter 4	Total
Increase in trade receivables	-$10	-$360	-$210	-$50	-$630
Increase in inventory	-5	-200	-105	-25	-335
Increase in trade payables	10	320	175	120	625
Net change	-$5	-$240	-$140	$45	-$340

The analysis reveals that Ninja is being forced to take on a large investment as a result of this new initiative, not only in additional accounts receivable, but also in inventory. This has created a bubble of new financing requirements that expanded rapidly in the second and third quarters, and appears to be tapering off in the fourth quarter. The company is clearly attempting to obtain a portion of the required funding by extending its payment terms with suppliers. Perhaps most troubling is the increase in trade payables in the fourth quarter, when there is no apparent need for it. It is possible that the company has been running short of cash at this point, and needs to extract even more money from its suppliers by delaying payments to them.

- *Lawsuit settlements.* If there are any funds received or paid out as the result of a lawsuit, these amounts are noted in a separate line item. It can be useful to add back lawsuit payouts from net income or subtract out from net income the effects of incoming lawsuit receipts, to gain a clearer view of the actual operating results of a business.
- *Cash flows for royalties and commissions.* A business may already be breaking out in its income statement any income or expenses related to royalties and commissions. If not, the information can be found here instead, and is useful for determining the extent to which these items play a role in a company's finances.

The items pointed out for further review are those not readily found elsewhere in the financial statements. For example, lawsuit settlements will probably be noted in the income statement, but may be aggregated into another line item, and so will be less identifiable.

Examination of Cash Flows from Investing Activities

As was the case with the cash flows from operating activities section, the investing activities part of the statement of cash flows suffers from an excessive degree of aggregation. Nonetheless, it is still possible to detect certain general directions in which management may be taking a company, as noted in the following bullet points:

- *Pre-growth build activities.* The total amount of fixed assets purchased is located in the investing activities section. This figure may have little relevance if a business has a pattern of acquiring fixed assets at a steady rate, year after year. However, in an asset-intensive industry, it may be possible to detect the ramp-up of corporate infrastructure leading to the launch of a new product line. This could be an especially interesting finding if there is a history of such asset purchases in the past, from which you might be able to estimate the future launch dates of new products. This interpretational tool would not work if a business outsources its production activities, since there would then be no fixed asset purchases to detect.
- *Outsourcing.* If there is a large sell-off of fixed assets, it can imply that management is planning to outsource certain asset-intensive parts of a business, such as its manufacturing capability. However, it could also mean that a business is simply cash-poor and needs the cash – which can be detected by examining the amount of cash on hand and the trend of debt acquisition.
- *Corporate takeovers.* One of the line items that may be used in the investing activities section is an aggregation of the debt or equity of other entities. While this amount is presented as an aggregated total, it can still be an indicator of the accumulation of the shares of a possible acquisition candidate, especially if the amount invested is unusually high in comparison to prior periods.

Examination of Cash Flows from Financing Activities

The nature of the line items used in the financing section makes this the most informative part of the statement of cash flows. There is a clear segregation of information among separate line items for dividends, stock sales, debt sales, stock repurchases, and so forth. This information can lead you to investigate the following topics:

- *Dividend trends.* The amount of dividends paid tends to be quite consistent over time. A key item to watch for is spikes in or the cancellation of dividends. A spike likely indicates a one-time special dividend, perhaps to pass through to investors a large gain experienced by the company. A dividend cancellation is a more significant issue to be aware of, since it can have several implications, such as:
  - That cash flows have weakened so much that the business can no longer afford to pay dividends

o That a major growth opportunity exists, which will be paid for by retaining the cash that would normally be distributed through dividends

- *Stock repurchases.* When there is a large stock repurchase, it can have several implications. One is that the repurchases are only triggered when a minimum stock price threshold has been reached – therefore, the stock is selling near the low end of its intended range. Another possibility is that a large investor has demanded a stock repurchase at a high price in order to stop threatening the company with a takeover attempt.

- *Stock and debt sales.* For smaller organizations, obtaining cash through the sale of debt or equity instruments is a relatively rare circumstance, which should certainly be noted when it appears in the statement of cash flows. In particular, determine the effect of any new fund raising on the debt-equity ratio of a business, which can be used to determine the riskiness of future debt repayments and whether it is even possible for an entity to raise any further debt funding. Additional debt is especially risky when the cash flows generated from operating activities are in decline, since this means a business is at greater risk of being unable to pay back the debt. A strong indicator of financial weakness is when a business is forced to sell preferred stock, since this usually means that investors want extra protection for their invested funds that gives them a priority over the holders of common stock.

- *Debt payments.* A key issue is whether a business has the financial resources to pay back its outstanding debt. The amount of these repayments is noted in the financial activities section. Watch this line item around the date of a debt maturity, to see if a business actually pays off the debt or instead rolls it forward into a new debt instrument.

- *Total changes.* Review the long-term trend of an organization's financing activities. If there are a continuing series of cash inflows from financing, there is a good chance that the business is in rapid growth mode, and needs cash from all possible sources in order to fund that growth. This is more likely to be the case if there is no evidence of dividends having been issued. Alternatively, if there is a long-term trend of paying off debt and/or buying back shares, it is reasonable to assume that the growth period is over, and the business is now generating excess funds. These are normal trends in the life cycle of a business. However, if sales and profits are declining and a business is still reporting a net inflow of cash from financing sources, this indicates that the business is inherently unprofitable, and perhaps should be shut down.

Summary

In this chapter, we have provided analysis tools for those investors who want to dig deeply into the financial statements issued by a business. A good source of additional information is the management's discussion and analysis section that accompanies all Form 10-K and 10-Q filings with the Securities and Exchange Commission, as well as the footnote disclosures contained within these filings. These additional disclosures can be surprisingly forthcoming in discussing the issues that a business is facing, as well as the new initiatives in which it is engaged.

Chapter 9
Investing Metrics

Introduction

A key concern of the investment community is whether to invest in the shares of a company, which involves multiple types of analysis. Investors are also interested in leading indicators of possible changes in the value of their shares, which they can use to decide whether to sell or hold the shares. In this chapter, we address a number of measurements that can assist in the investment decision, as well as other measures that can provide clues regarding future share prices.

Overview of Share Performance Measurements

In the following sections, we address several measurements that can be used to evaluate the price at which a share is currently selling. The price/earnings ratio compares the price of the stock to the most recently reported earnings of a business, while the capitalization rate derives the implied rate of return on share holdings. We also review the concept of total shareholder return, which compiles the total return for shareholders, based on dividends received and changes in the price of the stock.

We also look at the market value added concept, which calculates the difference between the market value of a business (i.e., the extended price at which all of its shares are currently selling) and the book value of invested capital. This measure provides a clue to the ability of management to generate value. A less-relevant (though common) measurement is the market to book ratio, which compares the market value of a business to its book value; the trouble is that book value is an accounting measure that may have little relevance when deriving the underlying value of a business.

We then turn to the prediction of the direction of a company's future stock price. One approach is the insider buy/sell ratio, under which the buying and selling activities of corporate insiders can be used to guesstimate whether insiders believe the current share price is too high or low. Another indicative measure is the options and warrants to common stock ratio; this ratio can be used to predict how many stock options and warrants may be converted to stock, which can in turn lead to a decline in the price of the stock, since more shares now have a claim on the residual value of a business. Yet another indicative measure is the short interest ratio, which quantifies the amount of interest by short sellers in a company's stock. Since short sellers usually conduct a deep investigation into the financial statements of a business, it is possible that a spike in short interest indicates problems that will lead to a stock price decline.

We conclude with the institutional holdings ratio, which measures the amount of a company's shares held by institutional investors in relation to the amount of trading volume. The outcome of this measurement is neither good nor bad; it merely reflects how large blocks of stock holdings can impact a variety of issues related to a business.

Price/Earnings Ratio

The price/earnings ratio is the price currently paid on the open market for a share of a company's stock, divided by its earnings per share. The ratio reveals the multiple of earnings that the investment community is willing to pay to own the stock. A very high multiple indicates that investors believe the company's earnings will improve dramatically, while a low multiple indicates the reverse. If the ratio is already high, there is little chance for the stock price to climb even higher, so there is significant risk that the share price will slide lower in the future. Historically, the price/earnings ratio for stocks traded in the United States has been about 15, so a ratio well above this figure probably indicates that a stock price cannot go much higher. However, an unusually low price/earnings ratio does not necessarily indicate a buying opportunity – it could mean that investors believe that a company is in trouble.

The investment community usually forces a stock price upward based on future expectations for such issues as new patents, new products, favorable changes in the laws impacting a company, and so forth.

To calculate the price/earnings ratio, divide the current market price per share by fully diluted earnings per share. The formula is:

$$\frac{\text{Current market price per share}}{\text{Fully diluted earnings per share}}$$

It is also possible to derive the ratio by dividing the total current company capitalization by net after-tax earnings. In this case, the formula is:

$$\frac{\text{Current company market capitalization}}{\text{Net after-tax earnings}}$$

Yet another variation is to build an expected price earnings ratio by dividing future earnings expectations per share into the current market price. This is not a firm indicator of where the ratio will actually be in the future, but is a good basis for deciding whether the stock is undervalued or overvalued.

There are several issues with the price/earnings ratio to be aware of. Consider the following problems:

- *Manipulation.* Earnings information can be manipulated by accelerating or deferring expense recognition, as well as through a variety of revenue recognition schemes. A more accurate measure of the value that the investment community is placing on a company's stock is the price to cash flow ratio. Cash flow is a good indicator of the results of operations.
- *Industry-wide effects.* Changes in the ratio tend to impact every company in an industry at the same time, because they are all subject to the same market forces, with slight differences between the various companies. Thus, a favorable change in the ratio may not be cause for excessive jubilation for a job

well done, since the change may not be traceable to a company's performance at all, but rather to changes in its business environment.

- *Timing*. The price of a company stock may fluctuate wildly in the short term, as such factors as takeover rumors and large customer orders excite investors and impact the price. Consequently, the ratio can be dramatically different if the timing of the measurement varies by just a few days.

EXAMPLE

The common stock of the Cupertino Beanery is currently selling for $15 per share on the open market. The company reported $3.00 of fully diluted earnings per share in its last annual report. Therefore, its price/earnings ratio is:

$$\frac{\$15 \text{ Market price per share}}{\$3 \text{ Earnings per share}}$$

$$= 5{:}1 \text{ Price/earnings ratio}$$

Capitalization Rate

It can be useful to derive the rate of return that investors expect on a company's stock, based on its current market price and the associated price/earnings ratio. We do this by simply reversing the price/earnings ratio, so that fully diluted earnings per share are divided by the current market price per share. The formula is:

$$\frac{\text{Fully diluted earnings per share}}{\text{Current market price per share}}$$

Since it contains the same information used for the price/earnings ratio noted in the last section, the capitalization rate should be considered to suffer from the same issues. Therefore, allow for possible manipulation of reported earnings, effects impacting the entire industry, and short-term variations in the price of the stock being examined.

EXAMPLE

A major institutional investor is interested in purchasing the shares of Atlas Machining Company, which has seen a major decline in its share price over the past year, due to concerns about its facilities in a country where there is a major ongoing insurgency. Despite the insurgency, Atlas has continued to report robust earnings of $3.50 per share in each of the last two years.

The investor's target rate of return on its investments is 15%. The capitalization rate for Atlas for the past two years is as follows:

	Last Year	Current Date
Earnings per share	$3.50	$3.50
Market price per share	$43.75	$21.88
Capitalization rate	8%	16%

The rapid drop in stock price has doubled the capitalization rate of Atlas over the past year, which makes this a reasonable investment opportunity that exceeds the investor's target rate of return.

Total Shareholder Return

When an investor buys the shares of a company, the return generated by the purchase will be derived from a combination of the change in the share price over the measurement period, plus any dividends paid by the company in the interim. The formula (on an annual basis) is noted in the following exhibit.

Total Shareholder Return Formula

	Ending stock price – Beginning stock price
+	Sum of all dividends received during the measurement period
=	Total shareholder return

The total return can then be divided by the initial purchase to arrive at a total shareholder return percentage.

This measurement can be skewed if a shareholder has control over a business. If this is the case and the company is sold, then the shareholder will likely be paid a control premium in exchange for giving up control over the entity.

EXAMPLE

An investor purchases shares of Albatross Flight Systems for $15.00 per share. One year later, the market value of the shares is $17.00, and the investor has received several dividends totaling $1.50. Based on this information, the total shareholder return is:

	$17.00 Ending stock price – $15.00 Beginning stock price
+	$1.50 Dividends received
=	$3.50 Total shareholder return

Based on the initial $15.00 purchase price, this represents a 23.3% total shareholder return.

Market Value Added

The market value added concept derives the difference between the market value of a business and its cost of invested capital. When market value is less than the cost of invested capital, this implies that management has not done a good job of creating value with the equity made available to it by investors. To derive market value added, follow these steps:

1. Multiply the total of all common shares outstanding by their market price.
2. Multiply the total of all preferred shares outstanding by their market price.
3. Combine these totals.
4. Subtract the amount of capital invested in the business.

The market value added formula appears in the following exhibit.

Market Value Added Formula

	(Number of common shares outstanding × Share price)
+	(Number of preferred shares outstanding × Share price)
-	Book value of invested capital
=	Market value added

This measurement should only be used if a company's stock is robustly traded on an established stock exchange. Otherwise, a few occasional trades could trigger substantial changes in the market price of the stock. It may be possible to derive the market value of shares by engaging an appraiser to provide an estimate.

Also, be aware that the current stock price may be based on changes in investor confidence in the market or industry as a whole, and do not relate to the performance (or lack thereof) of management in running a business.

EXAMPLE

The investor relations officer of Cud Farms is preparing a press release that reveals the increase in market value added since the new management team was hired. The analysis is based on the following information:

	Prior Year	Current Year
Number of common shares outstanding	5,000,000	5,700,000
Common stock price	$4.00	$4.20
Number of preferred shares outstanding	400,000	375,000
Preferred share price	$11.00	$11.30
Book value of invested capital	$18,000,000	$20,625,000

The market value added for the prior year is calculated as follows:

	(5,000,000 Common shares × $4.00 price)
+	(400,000 Preferred shares × $11.00 price)
-	$18,000,000 Equity book value
=	$6,400,000 Market value added

The market value added for the current year is calculated as follows:

	(5,700,000 Common shares × $4.20 price)
+	(375,000 Preferred shares × $11.30 price)
-	$20,625,000 Equity book value
=	$7,552,500 Market value added

Based on this analysis, the investor relations officer can highlight an increase of $1,152,500 in market value added since the new management team was hired.

Market to Book Ratio

A common measure of the value of a company's shares is the market to book ratio, which compares the market price of a company's stock to its book value per share. If the market price is well above the book value, this is said to be an indicator of the additional value that the investment community is placing on the ability of a company to earn a profit.

To calculate the market to book ratio, divide the ending price of the company's stock by the book value per share on the same date. The formula is:

$$\frac{\text{Ending market price of stock}}{\text{Book value per share}}$$

There are numerous problems with this measurement that limit its practical use. Consider the following issues:

- The comparison is of the market value of a business to the historical costs at which assets were recorded. There is no realistic reason why an asset base of any particular size should relate to a particular multiple of market price.
- Accounting standards mandate that some quite valuable intangible assets may not be recorded in the accounting records. In businesses where intangibles are the chief competitive advantage, this means that the market to book ratio will be inordinately high.
- Accounting standards mandate the use of accruals, reserves, and depreciation that can artificially alter the value of assets, irrespective of their real market value.

- The market price of the stock used in the numerator is as of a specific point in time, which may not closely relate to the average price of the stock in the recent past.

EXAMPLE

An analyst is reviewing the share performance of Failsafe Containment, which manufactures reactor vessels. The current market price of the company's stock is $20.00, and the book value per share is also $20.00, resulting in a market to book ratio of 1:1. However, further investigation reveals that the company has substantial real estate holdings, for which the recorded book value is substantially lower than their likely resale prices. Consequently, the analyst assigns a buy rating to the company's stock, which also attracts the attention of several corporate raiders that subsequently purchase the company and sell off the real estate for significant gains.

Insider Buy/Sell Ratio

In a publicly-held company, a large number of shares are typically held by corporate insiders. These insiders have the best access to information about the current and prospective performance of the business, and so are much more likely to sell their holdings when they believe the market price of the stock is likely peaking. Since these transactions must be reported to the Securities and Exchange Commission and are therefore public knowledge, it is not especially difficult for an outside investor to obtain and analyze stock transactions by insiders. The logic followed by an investor is that a high proportion of insider sales of company stock to insider purchases of stock is indicative of an insider belief that the stock price will go no higher. This information can be used by an investor to decide when to alter holdings of a company's stock.

To calculate the insider buy/sell ratio, aggregate the number of insider purchases of company stock over the measurement period, and divide by the aggregate amount of insider sales of company stock over the same period. The formula is:

$$\frac{\text{Aggregate insider stock purchases}}{\text{Aggregate insider stock sales}}$$

A ratio of less than one indicates that insiders believe that the price of the stock is peaking, while a ratio of greater than one indicates the reverse.

This is not an easy ratio to interpret, for corporate insiders may have excellent reasons for purchasing and selling company stock that have nothing to do with their perceptions of the company's prospects. Consider the following situations:

- A company recently went public, and many employees holding shares must wait six months before they are allowed to sell their shares. They will undoubtedly do so in six months.
- A newly-hired CEO is required to purchase $1 million of company shares as a condition of her employment.

- A CFO wants to purchase a new house, and sells enough shares to cover the purchase price of the home.
- Employees have such lucrative stock options pending that it would be foolish not to buy shares, irrespective of the future direction of the company's performance.

If the ratio is to be used as a valid indicator of the future direction in which the price of a stock may turn, consider the following situations that may be most applicable:

- There is a broad sell-off or purchasing pattern among multiple employees.
- Employees are incurring debt in order to buy shares.
- Employees in the accounting department, who presumably have the best understanding of company performance, are showing a decided buying or selling trend.

EXAMPLE

Six months have passed since Armadillo Industries went public. During the past week, Armadillo employees have finally had their shares registered, and have been actively liquidating their holdings in the company. An investor reviews the following information to see if there is a discernible trend in insider activity:

Employee Title	Transaction Type	Number of Shares	Transaction Date
Engineering manager	Sell	300,000	November 3
Marketing director	Sell	185,000	November 3
Chief financial officer	Buy	25,000	November 4
Chief information officer	Sell	160,000	November 4
Production manager	Sell	325,000	November 5
Chief executive officer	Buy	15,000	November 6
Controller	Buy	5,000	November 6

The information in the table results in an overwhelmingly negative insider buy/sell ratio of 0.046. However, the investor also notes that every one of the stock sale transactions involved a mid-level manager who might have simply been cashing in for the first time. All of the managers most closely associated with the company's finances are quietly buying up small blocks of stock. Based on his analysis of the information, and despite the outcome of the ratio, the investor believes that the company will report above-average results when its next quarterly results are released.

Options and Warrants to Common Stock Ratio

A company may elect to pay third parties with warrants for various services, and compensate its employees with stock options. If the business does so extensively, this can create an inordinately large pool of options and warrants that could be converted to common stock in the near future, resulting in significantly reduced earnings per share, and therefore a possible reduction in the stock price. Because of this dilutive effect, investors like to monitor the amount of outstanding options and warrants.

Investors will not consider all options and warrants to be convertible into common stock. Instead, they will focus on just those instruments that are currently "in the money," which means that the designated exercise price is below the current market price of a company's common stock. In this case, someone could (for example) exercise a stock option at a designated price of $5.00 and immediately earn a profit of $1.00 if the market price is $6.00. Conversely, if the market price were $5.00 or less, no option or warrant holder would find it profitable to purchase common stock with their instruments, and so would let them expire unused.

Given the importance of being in the money, an investor is only interested in these options and warrants, which may be far fewer than the total pool of options and warrants outstanding. Consequently, the calculation of options and warrants to common stock is to divide the grand total of in the money stock options and warrants by the total number of common shares currently outstanding. The formula is:

$$\frac{\text{Stock options in the money} + \text{Warrants in the money}}{\text{Total common shares outstanding}}$$

The measurement could be further refined to exclude those stock options that have not yet vested, since the holders of these options cannot yet exercise the options.

It may be useful to re-measure this ratio based on a modest prospective increase in the company's market price, rather than the current price. Doing so may significantly boost the number of shares beyond the level indicated by the initial measurement. This can warn investors that a run-up in the stock price could result in a large block of additional shares being issued.

EXAMPLE

Creekside Industrial has recently gone public through an initial public offering. An investor is reviewing the information submitted by Creekside to the Securities and Exchange Commission to ascertain the extent to which existing stock options and warrants may trigger the issuance of additional shares in the near future, thereby watering down the price of Creekside's stock. The investor finds the following information:

Common shares outstanding	50,000,000
Warrants in the money	1,000,000
Options in the money and vested	3,500,000
Options in the money and vesting in one year	750,000
Options in the money if price rises 20%	2,750,000
Options in the money if price rises 20%, and vesting in one year	10,000,000

The investor converts this information into a series of ratios that compare the options and warrants under various circumstances to common stock, which is noted in the following table:

[cumulative] (000s)	In the Money Now	Vesting in One Year	In the Money with 20% Price Increase	In the Money with 20% Increase & Vesting in 1 Year
Options and warrants	4,500	5,250	8,000	18,000
Number of common shares	50,000	50,000	50,000	50,000
Ratio	9%	11%	16%	36%

The investor notes that the amount of stock outstanding is likely to increase to a modest extent in the near future and in one year, but that the real risk is associated with a 20% increase in the price of Creekside's stock. If that happens, an additional 18,000,000 stock options will be in the money, which could result in a cumulative total of 36% of the existing balance of shares being issued. The investor concludes that any run-ups in the price of Creekside stock should be closely monitored.

Short Interest Ratio

Short sellers profit from declines in the price of a company's stock. They do so by examining the financial statements and prospects of a company in great detail; if they find a business whose prospects appear poor, or which seems to be inflating its financial results, then they target this entity for short selling. Short selling involves the sale of borrowed stock, which a short seller expects to buy later on the open market at a lower price, earning a profit on the decline in price.

It can be useful to track the interest of short sellers in a company's stock, since this can presage an abrupt decline in the price of that stock, especially once the short sellers begin to publicize their findings in an effort to create bearish sentiments about the stock. The easiest way to track short seller interest is through the short interest ratio. To calculate it, obtain the aggregate amount of short interest (which is available from several websites) and divide by the average daily trading volume for the stock. Short interest is the number of shares that investors have sold short, and which they have not yet closed out. The formula is:

$$\frac{\text{Short interest}}{\text{Average daily trading volume}}$$

The outcome of this analysis is the number of days that it would take short sellers to cover their positions in the company's stock, which they would likely have to do if the price of the company's shares starts to rise (since an increase in price generates losses for a short seller).

There are several analyses that can be derived from the short interest ratio. Consider the following situations:

- A prolonged and significant short interest ratio reveals a great deal of downward pressure on a stock by short sellers; however,
- When the ratio exceeds 2:1, short sellers will likely need to start buying shares in order to cover their positions, which can create a short-term spike in the stock price.
- Also, the ratio can be applied to entire industries, to see if short sellers are bearish on the fundamentals of an industry. If so, this is a strong indicator that stock prices will be flat or fall across the sector.

Institutional Holdings Ratio

The investors in a publicly-held company are typically comprised of a small number of institutional investors, such as pension funds, and a large number of retail investors (i.e., individuals). It is generally considered good to have a large proportion of institutional shareholders, for the following reasons:

- They indicate that a sophisticated investor is willing to buy into the company
- The investor relations department can more easily sell shares in large blocks to a small number of these investors
- The investor relations staff can more efficiently concentrate its publicity efforts on a small group of shareholders

However, institutional investors are not always a benefit to a company, for the following reasons:

- They can cause a major decline in a company's stock price if they decide to sell off their holdings over a short period of time
- They can use the voting power conveyed by their share holdings to pressure management to take certain actions, such as issuing dividends
- Their holdings can represent such a large part of the total pool of stock that the number of shares readily available for trading is relatively small

In short, there is no optimum level of institutional holdings to target. Instead, be aware of long-term trends in the activity ratio, and how this activity may impact the company's position in the public markets.

To calculate the institutional holdings ratio, divide the total trading volume by the period-end holdings of institutional investors. The measurement period is three months, since the holdings information comes from the Form 13F filings that institutional investors must file on a quarterly basis. The formula is:

$$\frac{\text{Total trading volume}}{\text{Institutional investor stockholdings}}$$

EXAMPLE

The Excalibur Shaving Company recently went public, selling a massive number of its shares to a small group of institutional investors. The trouble is that there are so few remaining shares that retail investors are complaining of an inability to trade their shares. Accordingly, the investor relations department contacts several institutional investors to see if they will part with some of their holdings. The results appear in the following table:

	One Month After IPO	Six Months After IPO
Total trading volume	2,500,000	10,000,000
Institutional investor stockholdings	50,000,000	30,000,000
Institutional holdings ratio	5%	33%

The table reveals that the investor relations department has succeeded in convincing some of the institutional investors to part with their shares, since the total holdings of this group have markedly declined. The change has resulted in a significant benefit, as activity in the company's stock has quadrupled.

Summary

The measurements addressed earliest in this chapter, such as the price/earnings ratio, can certainly give an investor a general feel for whether the shares of a company are over or undervalued. However, the decision to invest in a company should not be based on just the measurements noted in this chapter. Instead, a comprehensive review of both the financial and operational condition of a business should be conducted, as well as of the industry in which it operates, to arrive at a complete set of information that can be used as the basis for an investment decision.

We also noted that the measures used to indicate the future value of shares are highly interpretive. The inputs to these measurements should be closely examined before relying upon the measurements themselves. Also, these leading indicators are no match for a detailed and ongoing review of a business, so that all factors impinging on the ability of an organization to provide shareholder value are fully understood.

Glossary

B

Back-end load. A fee paid when selling mutual fund shares.

Balance sheet. A financial statement that presents information about an entity's assets, liabilities, and shareholders' equity.

Big bath. A large one-time write-off that management elects to take, usually in the form of a large reserve.

Bond. A fixed obligation to pay that is issued by a corporation or government entity to investors.

Book value. The amount of assets stated on an entity's balance sheet, minus the liabilities listed on the balance sheet.

C

Call option. A financial instrument that gives you the right, but not the obligation, to buy stock at a predetermined price within a specific range of dates.

Certificate of deposit. A term bank deposit with a fixed duration and a stated interest rate. In essence, it is a promissory note issued by a bank.

Collectibles. Items worth more than they were originally sold for, due to their rarity or popularity.

Contribution margin. Sales minus all variable expenses.

D

Discount broker. A stockbroker or brokerage firm that charges a reduced commission on transactions but typically does not provide investment advice or other services.

Dividend. A payment to shareholders of a portion of a corporation's earnings.

Dollar cost averaging. When you invest funds at a steady ready, using consistent timing.

E

Economic indicator. Economic data used to interpret the current or future state of the economy.

Exchange-traded fund. A fund that invests in a particular index, industry, or commodity.

F

Full-service broker. A brokerage firm that provides the full range of services to its clients, such as retirement and tax planning, as well as analysis reports on various securities.

H

Hedge fund. A fund that pools the money of contributing investors and tries to achieve above-market returns through a wide variety of investment strategies.

I

Income statement. A financial statement that contains the results of an organization's operations for a specific period of time, showing revenues and expenses and the resulting profit or loss.

Individual retirement account. A savings account with tax advantages that individuals can open to save and invest over the long term.

Intangible asset. A non-physical asset that has a useful life spanning more than one accounting period.

Investing. The act of allocating resources with the expectation of generating a profit.

L

Leading indicator. An economic indicator that predicts future economic activity levels.

Limit order. An order to buy or sell a stock, but only if the transaction can be completed at a specific price or better.

Liquidity. The ease with which an asset or security can be converted into cash.

M

Marginal tax rate. The amount of additional tax paid for every additional dollar earned as income.

Market order. An order to buy or sell a stock at the best available price.

Money market fund. A type of mutual fund that restricts its investments to highly liquid, near-term instruments.

Mutual fund. A type of financial vehicle that is made up of a pool of money obtained from a large number of investors; its goal is to invest the money in a variety of securities, as stated in its prospectus.

P

Penny stock. A small company's stock that trades for less than $5 per share, and which trades over-the-counter.

Put option. A contract that gives its holder the right, but not the obligation, to sell stock at a strike price, before the option's expiration date.

S

Sales load. The commission charged to an investor when buying shares in a mutual fund.

SEC yield. A calculation that approximates the yield an investor would receive in a year by assuming that bonds in the portfolio are held to maturity, all income reinvested, and all fees and expenses factored in.

Shares. Units of stock.

Speculative bubble. A spike in asset value that is fueled by irrational speculative activity that is not supported by the fundamentals.

Sprint capacity. Production capacity upstream from the bottleneck operation in the production area.

Statement of cash flows. A financial statement that identifies the different types of cash payments made by a business to third parties, as well as payments made to a business by third parties.

Stock. A security that represents the ownership of a fraction of a corporation. This ownership interest entitles the owner to a proportion of the firm's assets and profits.

Stock index. A group of shares that are used to give an indication of the stock market as a whole or a subset of it.

Stock market. The collection of exchanges at which the shares of publicly-traded companies are bought and sold.

Stockbroker. A financial professional who executes buy and sell orders in the market on behalf of clients.

V

Value averaging. Similar to dollar cost averaging, but you would buy more shares when prices are falling, and fewer shares when prices are increasing.

W

Wash sale rule. A rule which states that a taxpayer cannot claim a loss on the sale or trade of a security if it is replaced with a substantially identical security within 30 days.

Y

Yield curve. A graphical representation of the yields on a bond, based on its maturity date.

Index

www.ingramcontent.com/pod-product-compliance
Lightning Source LLC
Chambersburg PA
CBHW051347200326
41521CB00014B/2510